INSIGHT ⊙ GUIDES

EXPLORE

ORLANDO

⊙ Walking Eye App

Your guide now includes a free eBook to your chosen destination, for the same great price as before. Simply download the Walking Eye App from the App Store or Google Play to access your free eBook.

HOW THE WALKING EYE APP WORKS

Through the Walking Eye App, you can purchase a range of eBooks and destination content. However, when you buy this book, you can download the corresponding eBook for free. Just see below in the grey panel where to find your free content and then scan the QR code at the bottom of this page.

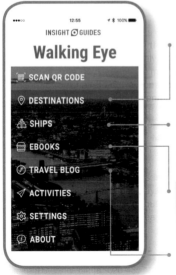

Destinations: Download essential destination content featuring recommended sights and attractions, restaurants, hotels and an A–Z of practical information, all available for purchase.

Ships: Interested in ship reviews? Find independent reviews of river and ocean ships in this section, all available for purchase.

eBooks: You can download your free accompanying digital version of this guide here. You will also find a whole range of other eBooks, all available for purchase.

Free access to travel-related blog articles about different destinations, updated on a daily basis.

HOW THE EBOOKS WORK

The eBooks are provided in EPUB file format. Please note that you will need an eBook reader installed on your device to open the file. Many devices come with this as standard, but you may still need to install one manually from Google Play.

The eBook content is identical to the content in the printed guide.

HOW TO DOWNLOAD THE WALKING EYE APP

1. Download the Walking Eye App from the App Store or Google Play.
2. Open the app and select the scanning function from the main menu.
3. Scan the QR code on this page – you will then be asked a security question to verify ownership of the book.
4. Once this has been verified, you will see your eBook in the purchased ebook section, where you will be able to download it.

Other destination apps and eBooks are available for purchase separately or are free with the purchase of the Insight Guide book.

CONTENTS

ANIMAL LOVERS

Let sharks, penguins, and other marine creatures entertain you at SeaWorld (route 7), see exotic animals along jungle trails at Disney's Animal Kingdom (route 4), and go on a Serengeti Safari at Busch Gardens (route 15).

RECOMMENDED ROUTES FOR...

ART BUFFS

Browse the art galleries in Downtown Orlando (route 8), visit the Mennello Museum and Orlando Museum of Art in Loch Haven Park (route 9), the Morse Museum in Winter Park (route 12), and the Dalí Museum in Tampa Bay (route 15).

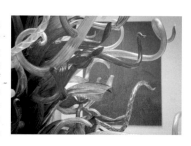

CHILDREN

Step into storybook worlds at the Magic Kingdom's Fantasyland (route 1) and Islands of Adventure's Seuss Landing (route 6). Learn while playing at SeaWorld (route 7) and the Orlando Science Center (route 9), but save time for LEGOLAND Florida (route 11).

ESCAPING THE CROWDS

Go beachcombing on the sandy stretches of Cocoa Beach (route 14) or Fort De Soto Park (route 15). Explore the trails at Wekiwa Springs, Blue Springs State Park, or Merritt Island (routes 13 and 14).

FOODIES

Munch your way around the world at Epcot's World Showcase (route 2). Visit some of the city's best restaurants in Downtown Orlando (route 8) and Winter Park (route 12).

MOVIE LOVERS

Put yourself in the middle of Harry Potter's Wizarding World at Universal Orlando (route 5) or be immersed in larger-than-life classic film scenes on the Great Movie Ride at Disney Hollywood Studios (route 3).

NATURE LOVERS

Take an airboat ride on Lake Toho (route 11), see manatees in the wild at Blue Springs State Park (route 13), go canoeing on the Hillsborough River or Wekiwa Springs (routes 15 and 13), or spot wildlife at Merritt Island National Refuge (route 14).

SHOPPERS

International Drive (route 10) is a shopper's gateway to designer outlet stores. Go souvenir hunting along Highway 192 in Kissimmee (route 11) or escape the chains on frou-frou Park Avenue in Winter Park (route 12).

INTRODUCTION

An introduction to Orlando's geography, customs and culture, plus illuminating background information on cuisine, history, and what to do when you're there.

EXPLORE ORLANDO

With eight major theme parks, several water parks, a myriad cultural and other attractions, and the second-largest convention center in the country, Orlando is a huge tourist destination, attracting 68 million visitors a year.

The city of Orlando lies at the heart of Central Florida's largest metropolitan region. Although it measures only 65 sq miles (168 sq km) in Orange County, Greater Orlando covers 2.6 million acres (1.04 million hectares) in adjoining Osceola, Seminole and Lake counties. It encompasses the cities of Kissimmee to the south, Winter Park and Maitland to the north and, to the southwest, Walt Disney World Resort, which in fact has its own government body. However, there's much more to Orlando than the theme parks that made it famous, from art and cultural offerings to its wildlife and lush environment.

LAKES AND RIVERS

Orlando's landscape is largely flat, and as the city expanded much of the terrain was drained from the natural swamps and wetlands. There are more than 2000 lakes, rivers, and springs in Greater Orlando. Shingle Creek, Boggy Creek and other channels form part of a vast watershed that runs all the way to the Everglades.

Dozens of lakes are dotted throughout the urban areas, from Lake Eola in down-town Orlando, to big Lake Toho in Kissimmee, to tiny Lake Lily in Maitland (site of a local Sunday farmers' market) to Winter Park's chain of lakes connected by scenic canals. Wildlife is perfectly at home in this urban environment, and you'll regularly see heron, egrets, storks, wildfowl, turtles, and even alligators.

CITY LAYOUT

Downtown Orlando, the city's commercial center, lies several miles north of the theme parks and Convention Center. Interstate 4 (I-4) is the main thoroughfare that links the various parts. It stretches from Tampa Bay on the Gulf Coast northeast through Orlando to Daytona Beach. I-4 runs north and south in Orlando, but runs east to west from end to end, so use this guide while in town: east means north; west means south. This major artery will be undergoing construction work until at least 2021, so check for traffic reports. Beyond I-4, Orlando's major thoroughfares are either busy roads with traffic lights or well-maintained, practically traffic-free toll roads. Highway 528, a toll road also known as the Beachline

Downtown Orlando at sunset

Expressway, runs from I-4 east to Cocoa Beach. The Central Florida Greenway, 417, runs along the east end of town and reaches down to near Celebration. The 429 travels from Apopka south to Kissimmee, passing the western edge of Disney World. In the tourist corridors, International Drive serves the Convention Center as well as many attractions. Highway 192 in Kissimmee, with its proximity to Disney World, is another major tourist thoroughfare. In Lake Buena Vista, Apopka-Vineland Road/535 is the main road.

RURAL ROOTS

Long before Walt Disney arrived and changed the face of Orlando forever, this was cattle and citrus country. From 1920 to 1954, Dr Philip Phillips was the world's largest citrus-grower, with more than 5,000 acres (2,000 hectares) of groves in Orange County. He introduced crop-dusting by plane, and perfected a way to make canned orange juice taste good.

It may be hard to find an orange tree – let alone a grove – in the city today (except at 'U-Pick' groves in the suburbs, a great way to feast on citrus straight from the tree), but special events pay homage to Orlando's rural roots. More than 100,000 oranges, grapefruits and tangerines adorn colorful floats that wind through Downtown during the annual Florida Citrus Parade, held at the end of December. The Silver Spurs Rodeo, which takes place twice a year in Kissimmee, bills itself as the largest rodeo east of the Mississippi.

PEOPLE

Orlando is a young town. Of the nearly 2.4 million people who live in the metropolitan region, the median age is only about 37. People relocate here from all over the country, and it's estimated that over 60,000 new residents arrive every year. In fact, the population of the metropolitan area has leapt from 1.6 million in 2000 to 2.4 million in 2016.

Disney is of course the top employer with 74,000 'cast members' – Universal Orlando is the second, with 21,000 employees – but the area also boasts many high-tech companies and major industries including digital media, aviation, aerospace, accounting, and biomedicine. Dozens of international firms also have branches here, and more than 25 of the largest have their headquarters in town. And with 64,000 students, the University of Central Florida in Orlando is one of America's largest universities.

THEME PARKS AND ATTRACTIONS

Walt Disney World Resort
Walt Disney World Resort (www.disney world.com) is actually located outside the city limits of Orlando, in the cities of Lake Buena Vista and Bay Lake. Covering more than 25,000 acres (101 sq km), it is made up of four theme parks (the Magic Kingdom, Epcot, Disney's Animal

Orlando Museum of Art

Kingdom, and Disney's Hollywood Studios), two water parks (Typhoon Lagoon and Blizzard Beach), the Disney Springs dining/shopping/entertainment district, Disney's Wide World of Sports complex, other sports facilities from golf courses to a water-skiing area, about three dozen resort hotels, two spas, a wedding pavilion, and even a campground. It really is a world in itself.

Disney Springs

Spread along a lake shore and covering 120 acres (50 hectares), Disney

The Kennedy Space Center   *Universal Orlando Resort after dark*

Springs (www.disneysprings.com) consists of four parts. West Side focuses on dining and entertainment, with cinemas, House of Blues, Splitsville for a bowling/dining/drinking combo, and restaurants such as Planet Hollywood Observatory (with sandwiches by celebrity chef Guy Fieri and a domed ceiling displaying high-definition video). The Landing is chockful of big-name restaurants like Morimoto Asia and Chef Art Smith's Homecoming Kitchen – both with inexpensive take-out-window options that include adult beverages, plus the grand Irish pub Raglan Road and free outdoor musical entertainment. Town Center is a spiffy, upscale, open-air mall with brand-name boutiques, plus Mexican fare from Chicago chef Rick Bayless at Frontera Cocina. Marketplace is geared for shopping and also has several more restaurants. There is no admission fee to the complex; hours vary by location.

Universal Orlando Resort
Universal Orlando Resort (www.universalorlando.com) is located in central Orlando between the Convention Center and Downtown. It comprises two theme parks – Universal Studios Florida and Islands of Adventure, which between them have two sections replicating parts of Harry Potter's world. The complex also includes a water park called Volcano Bay, and five on-site resort hotels (with a sixth scheduled to debut in 2018).

CityWalk
On the waterfront between Universal Studios and Islands of Adventure is CityWalk, a dining and nightlife complex with a plethora of themed bars, restaurants, and nightclubs. In addition to taking in shows at a Hard Rock arena and a Blue Man Group venue, you can dine at restaurants ranging from the world's largest Hard Rock Café and Pat O'Brien's Orlando (styled after the famous New Orleans original) to sophisticated Emeril's Orlando, and trendy Cowfish with sushi and burgers. The Toothsome Chocolate Emporium & Savory Feast Kitchen offers meals and sweets. Bob Marley and The Groove nightclub attract a 21-plus crowd.

'Tin can tourists'

Central Florida's tourism boom actually started long before Disney. In the 1920s, paved roads and Model-T Fords opened up the region's natural attractions to 'tin can tourists'. They drove south on the Dixie Highway, their cars rigged up with folding side tents, to enjoy the weather and such early attractions as alligator wrestling at Gatorland and dancing mermaids at Weeki Wachee Springs. Their name referred to the cars and the food they ate from tinned cans – they were notorious for their frugality. Governor Fuller Warren said of them: 'They came to Florida with one suit of underwear and one $20 bill, and changed neither.'

Preparing for Mickey's Not-So-Scary Halloween Party

You can visit CityWalk separately from the parks; there is no admission fee apart from cover charges at some music clubs. It is open from 11am until 2am.

SeaWorld

SeaWorld (www.seaworldparks.com) is located in central Orlando, along I-Drive south of the Convention Center. Across the street its smaller sister park, Discovery Cove, offers a more intimate encounter with marine animals. The Aquatica water park opened next door in 2008. All three are owned by SeaWorld Entertainment, Inc., which also operates the Busch Gardens theme park in Tampa.

LEGOLAND Florida

Those colorful kid-friendly blocks are the foundation of LEGOLAND Florida Resort (www.legoland.com/florida), a theme-park complex an hour south of downtown Orlando, geared towards families with children aged two to 12. The 150-acre (60-hectare) attraction has rides aplenty, broken into sections like Fun Town, Miniland USA (with a Star Wars section), LEGO Kingdoms, and LEGO Technic. Toddlers will most enjoy the DUPLO section, based around bigger blocks. A LEGO-themed water park and two hotels are also located on-site.

The big splash

When the temperature rises, cool off in the resorts' themed water parks. Disney's Typhoon Lagoon is a topsy-turvy paradise left in the wake of a tropical storm. It features a variety of water slides, a huge surf pool, and a chance to snorkel with the sharks at Shark Reef. The newest addition, Miss Adventure Falls, is a family raft ride involving a shipwreck. And only Disney could imagine Blizzard Beach, a summer ski resort created by a freak Florida snowstorm. Among its watery thrill rides is the Summit Plummet, a 120ft (36-meter) vertical free-falling body slide from the top of Mt Gushmore.

Aquatica is SeaWorld's water park. True to form, the first slide you come to is the Dolphin Plunge, which shoots you right through a pool of Commerson's dolphins. With their black and white markings, they look like miniature killer whales. The park has some thrilling water slides too, along with a relaxing beach, huge surf pool, a lazy river and colorful kiddie play areas (see page 62).

In mid-2017, Universal Orlando opened the doors to Volcano Bay, a 28-acre (11-hectare) water park with 18 themed areas. Some attractions are classic body and raft slides, while others are more innovative.

LEGOLAND has its own water park too, tailored for school-age kids with a wave pool, lazy river, and a place to build your own LEGO raft.

Busch Gardens in Tampa also has an adjoining water park, Adventure Island (www.adventureisland.com), open March–October.

The Manta roller coaster at SeaWorld twists and turns like the ray

TOP TIPS FOR VISITING ORLANDO

Stay cool. The dazzling Florida summer sun and sweltering heat are dangerous. Apply sunscreen regularly, wear a wide-brimmed hat, and seek out shade or air conditioning at regular intervals.

Be water-safe. Watch children vigilantly, even if they're wearing floatees and a lifeguard is present. A couple dozen children – mostly toddlers, but teens too – drown every year in Florida.

Embrace day trips. Rent a car, or sign up for a tour, and explore. Atlantic coast beaches are 50 miles (80km) away, Gulf Coast strands 75 miles (120km). Multi-ethnic Miami (230 miles/370km), old-money West Palm Beach (166 miles/270km), rural Lake Okeechobee (108 miles/174km), and historic St Augustine (100 miles/160km) beckon too.

Go grocery shopping. Pick up foodstuffs and prepared meals at Publix supermarkets, which has a good deli with online ordering. For more upscale items, visit FreshMarket or Whole Foods.

Attend special events. Epcot's lengthy International Food and Wine Festival, held every autumn, is loaded with ethnic food kiosks, chef talks, wine tastings, cooking classes, and special dinners. Other highlights: springtime's Epcot International Flower & Garden Festival, and winter's Epcot International Festival of the Arts.

Seek out themed evenings. Book an evening at the Magic Kingdom's Mickey's Not-So-Scary Halloween Party or Mickey's Very Merry Christmas Party. In addition to wonderful theming and complimentary treats, both are refreshingly free of crowds. At Universal Orlando, themed evenings are more adult-oriented. Experience a replica of music-happy Mardi Gras in winter/spring and the frightening thrills of Halloween Horror Nights in autumn.

Peek behind the scenes. Universal's personalized VIP tours take you deep behind the scenes – and to the front of the line for attractions. Disney's line-up ranges from 'backstage' walk-throughs to a safari experience.

Get app-happy. Each theme-park complex, and Visit Orlando, have free smartphone apps that may assess attraction wait times, reserve restaurant tables, and way more.

Dine well for less. Each September, dozens of Orlando's top restaurants sell three-course dinners for $33 via Magical Dining Month. The rest of the year, visit for lunch, when prices are usually lower. For chain bargains, look for coupons in brochures, flyers, and tourist magazines.

Schedule your meals. American meal times are earlier than in Europe. Most restaurants open for lunch around 11 or 11.30am and serve until around 2.30pm. Dinner hours are generally from 4 or 4.30pm until 10 or 11pm. Waits of an hour or more are common in high-traffic areas. Make a reservation if possible – www.opentable.com is helpful, or come early or late.

Fresh seafood

FOOD AND DRINK

It's not all fast food on the tourist trail. Orlando has a deliciously broad dining scene, from casual, inexpensive eateries to upscale, romantic restaurants with top chefs at the helm. You'll find regional specialties, too – gator tail, anyone?

CULINARY INFLUENCES

Around the world

Orlando's outlook on cuisine is increasingly international. While all-American burgers and fries are seemingly everywhere, look around and you'll find authentic foods from every corner of the world, from Cuba to France, Ethiopia to Peru. Tapas (or 'small plates') restaurants are highly popular, some featuring the foods of Spain, others mixing and matching global flavors. The Mills 50 district has an enclave of Asian restaurants. All over town, pizza is easy to find, as are Italian staples. Options range from cozy family-owned joints to upscale restaurants serving first-class international dishes.

Down home

With its roots firmly in the South, Orlando has a variety of restaurants serving Southern specialties. Traditional 'Cracker' food generally involves fried catfish, alligator, and frogs' legs. Homier Deep South fare like grits, cornbread, and fried chicken with 'sweet tea' can be found in certain casual restaurants. Gussied-up versions often appear in higher-end establishments, where pecan-crusted pork and hand-crafted bourbon cocktails flaunt the area's Southern roots. While most Southern regions have their own barbecued-meat style, Orlando doesn't, but many small local chains take the best of styles around the country. And for dessert, many Orlando restaurants offer personal versions of Key lime pie, a specialty from the southernmost tip of the Florida peninsula.

Tropical tastes

The Caribbean influence is unmistakeable too, and you can experience that in two ways: in humble, authentic hideaways frequented by residents, and in lively tourist-oriented restaurants with festive decor, oversized fruity drinks, and upbeat music designed to create a tropical vibe. In the more Americanized places, coconut shrimp is popular as either a starter or main course, mango salsa as a condiment.

The pride of the USA

Ever-popular American steaks and burgers are ubiquitous all around Orlando, in establishments that vary greatly in price and quality. Luckily, Orlando's chefs

Ever-popular key lime pie

Creative burgers at Epcot

have begun getting competitive about their burgers, creating especially juicy and flavorful versions. And with both the Atlantic and the Gulf coasts a stone's throw away, it's not surprising that fish and seafood are highly prevalent too, though they're not necessarily inexpensive. The area has quite a few vegetarian and vegan restaurants too. Most table-service restaurants offer several choices of fresh salads, which come in big portions with protein options including shrimp and chicken.

PLACES TO EAT

Like any large city, Orlando has its hip dining areas. Mills 50 has a range of walk-in joints specializing in Asian food. Downtown's Church Street Station has a handful of creative restaurants offering everything from farm-to-table American cuisine to Spanish-style tapas. Thornton Park and College Park, east and west of Downtown respectively, both have several contemporary restaurants with an urban bistro atmosphere. Winter Park is a long-established favorite for its upscale, quality restaurants, many with sidewalk seating that offers terrific people-watching. Celebration's main roads are lined with a variety of family-friendly places. The small, historic outskirt cities of Winter Garden and Sanford are abloom with popular new eateries and craft-beer purveyors. You needn't travel far from the theme parks and Convention Center, though. Sand Lake Road,

Orlando's 'Restaurant Row,' is lined with higher-end chains and several independent restaurants of assorted cuisines.

Chain restaurants

Plenty of chain restaurants offer the familiar to visitors seeking what they already know. Unsurprisingly, they are most prevalent along the main tourist drags such as Highway 192, 535/Apopka-Vineland in Lake Buena Vista, and International Drive. All the usual fast-food suspects are here, as are mid-pricers such as Applebee's, Outback, and Olive Garden, offering a much wider menu. Stalwarts like International House of Pancakes (IHOP) and Denny's serve all-day (or all-night) breakfasts. Fast-casual concepts have proliferated of late, inviting guests to stand at a counter while a tailored meal is prepared to order. Chipotle does this with Southwestern fare, Spoleto with pasta, MidiCi with pizza, and Pei Wei with Asian flavors. At the fancier end, Orlando's tourist strips are home to chains like Eddie V's, the healthy food-oriented Seasons 52, and, for seafood, Ocean Prime and Oceanaire – plus just about every high-end steakhouse chain in the country.

Buffet restaurants

If you're looking for a bargain, look no further than one of Orlando's many buffet restaurants. They range from Chinese smorgasbords to all-you-can-eat steak and salad bars, Indian lunch buffets, and even lobster feasts.

Steakhouses

The sheer number of independent and chain steakhouses makes Orlando a carnivore's delight. Here, as with seafood, you get what you pay for. Several inexpensive steakhouse chains with big salad bars cater to families on a budget. If you're a real steak-lover, give them a miss and go for the higher-end, quality restaurants, of which there are several. They offer hand-cut, wet- or dry-aged prime beef, oak-grilled, flame-broiled or otherwise cooked to perfection. Most steakhouses also serve a selection of fine seafood. Bull & Bear in the Waldorf Astoria, and Spencer's in The Hilton Orlando, are especially good.

High-end restaurants

With dozens of upscale restaurants within a 10-mile (16-km) radius of the Orange County Convention Center, diners will find plenty of choices for a memorable meal in Orlando. Several, especially in the tourist corridors, are overseen by internationally acclaimed or celebrity chefs. Among the biggies represented here are Masaharu Morimoto, Melissa Kelly, Art Smith, Rick Bayless, Emeril Lagasse, Todd English, and Norman Van Aken.

Local stars

Look beyond the big-name brands and you'll find a vibrant community of exceptional restaurants, bistros and gastropubs owned and run by local chefs, many of them recognized by the prestigious James Beard Foundation. Mostly in Orlando and Winter Park, top-quality ingredients, scratch cooking and hand-crafted cocktails are part of the draw.

Food halls

As artisan foodstuffs gain popularity, Orlando's two food halls have become gathering spots for dining on fresh local foods in a simple space, and sipping smoothies and beers. East End Market in Orlando's Audubon Park Garden District, and Plant Street Market in Winter Garden, both draw mellow crowds for their variety, rustic charm, and communal outdoor seating.

Theme park and resort dining

Though the choice of food is wide, the quality varies enormously at Orlando's theme parks. At the lower end of the scale, the food is often overpriced for what can turn out to be mediocre, mass-produced fare. Go up a notch or two and you can enjoy some excellent meals. It's tough if you only have a day at a park and want to make the most of the attractions rather than spending time on a sit-down meal. The exception is Epcot's World Showcase,

Craft beer on tap in Winter Garden

where some of the quick, lower-priced options are especially interesting.

The parks really excel in themed dining and decor. You can sit beside a coral reef or a shark tank, in an African setting, or even in an Irish pub. In all of the theme-park complexes, you can find restaurants to dine with popular characters for breakfast, lunch, or dinner. This is a big hit with families, but should be booked well in advance. The princess character meals at Cinderella's Royal Table in the Magic Kingdom, and at Akershus Royal Banquet Hall in Epcot's Norway pavilion, are especially popular. At Universal, favorites including The Simpsons enliven meals. The best range of themed restaurants at all price levels can be found in Orlando's two dining/shopping/entertainment enclaves: Disney Springs and Universal's CityWalk (see page 56).

Several resort restaurants at the upper end rate among the top fine-dining spots in Orlando, including those in the Disney's Grand Floridian, Animal Kingdom Lodge, and BoardWalk Inn.

DRINKS

Alcoholic drinks

Orlando has all sorts of interesting places to raise a glass of your favorite tipple, from classy lounges to intimate martini spots to dazzling nightclubs. There are piano bars with dueling pianos and sing-alongs, trendy cigar bars, raucous sports bars, and nightspots offering blues, jazz, and rock 'n' roll. A number of bars have Happy Hour specials on cocktails and bottled beers.

Restaurants and bars often have extensive wine lists with European as well as New World wines. For wine lovers, Funky Monkey at Pointe Orlando, the Eola Wine Company (Downtown), and The Wine Room in Winter Park offer fine wines by the glass.

The popularity of micro-breweries has greatly increased the choice of quality beers. Among your choices are The Bear & Peacock, Crooked Can, and Ocean Sun. Craft cocktails are also big in Orlando. Some of the more serious cocktail bars even display jars of locally grown herbs to show how fresh the ingredients are. The Courtesy Bar, Herman's Loan Office, and The Bakery Bar are all good bets.

Always take photo identification that gives your birthdate if you want to enjoy an alcoholic drink. You must be 21 years old to drink, and be able to prove it.

Coffee and tea

Orlando is a coffee-savvy city. Here, even hotel breakfast buffets often offer quality brands in different strengths to suit everyone's tastes. Super-serious coffee shops include Foxtail Coffee, Lineage Coffee Roasting, Axum Coffee, and Downtown Credo.

You can get hot tea at most cafés and restaurants, and green tea and herbal teas are widely available. Iced tea is an American favorite and, like filter coffee, often comes with free refills. It's often served already sweetened.

Saks Off 5th at Orlando Premium Outlet

SHOPPING

If you're looking for clever character-based merchandise or designer discounts, Orlando is a shopper's paradise. The town is loaded with retailers, from mega-malls with the latest fashions to outlet centers with top-name brands at discounted prices.

Orlando's souvenir specialty is theme-park specific. Each park has hats, T-shirts, and way more featuring their choice characters. Exit any thrill ride and you're bound to find versions boasting kudos for 'surviving'. Or, for a taste of Old Florida, seek out one of the remaining citrus stands and buy a crate of oranges or pink grapefruits grown in a local grove – no need to carry it onto the plane; most will happily ship the citrus for you.

Still, Orlando's main draw for shoppers is its grand share of national and international chains, both in enclosed retail malls and open-air outlet centers – not to mention yet more in strip malls all over town. These malls often have special deals for international tourists, so be sure to visit the customer-service desk and ask questions.

elers. Among the 150 other stores, though, are appealing chain stores with moderately priced merchandise.

The Florida Mall (8001 S. Orange Blossom Trail) is larger, with 250 specialty shops and department stores including its own Macy's, plus Dillard's and value-priced Sears and JCPenney. Its Crayola Experience, Build-a-Bear Workshop, American Girl, and M&M's World make it appealing to families.

The section of International Drive near the Convention Center continues to grow, and shoppers find ways to max out their credit cards at Pointe Orlando (9101 International Drive) and I-Drive 360, both loaded with shops, boutiques, and restaurants along with tourist attractions. Yet more shelves will be stocked when the SKYPLEX Entertainment Complex debuts in 2019.

MALLS AND SHOPPING CENTERS

Orlando's most special mall is the Mall at Millenia (4200 Conroy Road), which is anchored by luxury retailers Neiman Marcus, Bloomingdale's, and Macy's. Its halls are rich with showrooms by renowned designers and upscale jew-

OUTLET STORES

Cameras, clothing, luggage, sporting goods, even perfumes – you name it, there's a discount outlet for it somewhere in Orlando.

For the most appealing way to seek out those bargains, head to one

ETs waiting for a new home   *Zara at Disney Springs*

of three open-air outlet malls that between them feature hundreds of stores with name-brand merchandise. Orlando International Premium Outlets (4951 International Drive) includes Neiman Marcus Last Call and Saks Off 5th, plus couture brands like Ted Baker and St. John. At the southern end of International Drive, Orlando Vineland Premium Outlets (8200 Vineland Avenue) and its outparcels have some of the same big names plus others like Elie Tahari, Lululemon, and Tommy Bahama. The smaller Lake Buena Vista Factory Stores nearby (15657 Apopka Vineland Road) features Eddie Bauer, Tommy Hilfiger, Gap and Oshkosh B'Gosh among its outlets.

Some are true outlets, others 'company stores', but all offer discounts of 25–75 percent. Be aware that the merchandise often differs from the fashions at the regular stores. When buying at the outlet centers, particularly electronic equipment, it pays to know your merchandise and prices, and to avoid being talked into buying alternatives.

In addition to the mega outlet malls, strip malls and even freestanding bargain stores line the main tourist drag of Highway 192 and the stretch of I-Drive north of Sand Lake Road.

SOUVENIRS

It's hard to walk away from the theme parks without a memorable charac-ter T-shirt or cuddly toy in hand. Every theme park sells wonderfully creative merchandise. In addition, the Disney Springs and CityWalk complexes at Disney World and Universal Orlando respectively are packed with clothing, jewelry, and souvenir stores, both with free admission. Disney Springs' World of Disney is a treasure chest of take-home goods, and surrounding stores sell specialty items from collectible pins to kitchenware, Disney art and trendy clothing. The Universal Studios Store at CityWalk has similarly themed merchandise playing up that complex's characters, including Woody Woodpecker and Dr. Seuss's Thing One and Thing Two – a favorite for siblings. For a bargain, check out Disney's Character Warehouse at Orlando Premium Outlets and the Theme Park Outlet at Lake Buena Vista Factory Stores.

BOUTIQUES

While the town has few boutiques, the determined visitor seeking unusual goods can find personable boutique stores scattered among the neighborhoods. The Sand Lake Road area between Turkey Lake Road and Apopka-Vineland Road has fun women's apparel boutiques tucked between the 'Restaurant Row' eateries. Winter Park boasts the greatest concentration of independent retailers along Park Avenue, with a few more on Orlando Avenue, especially in Winter Park Village.

A 1650s Native American village

HISTORY: KEY DATES

Long before Europeans appeared on the scene, central Florida was the domain of the Timucua Indians. The Spanish, French, and British battled it out for centuries, but it is now Walt Disney who reigns supreme.

EARLY HISTORY

15,000–7,500 BC	Ice Age glaciers drive Paleo-Indian hunters southwards to the Florida peninsula.
7,500–5,000 BC	North America's first human burials near Cape Canaveral.

COLONIAL TIMES

1498	John and Sebastian Cabot make first European sighting of Florida.
1513	Juan Ponce de León claims Cape Canaveral for Spain.
1562	French settlers build a fort on the St Johns River but are driven out by the Spanish, who found St Augustine.
mid-1700s	Creek Indians – dubbed Seminoles – and runaway African slaves are driven south by American settlers into Florida.
1764–83	Britain rules Florida for 19 years before it is returned to Spain.
1818	First Seminole War; US General Andrew Jackson campaigns against the Indians in order to take control of Florida.
1819	Spain cedes Florida to the US.
1821–42	Second Seminole War; Seminole leader Osceola is imprisoned and dies a martyr in 1838. Seminoles are driven into the Everglades or relocated to reservations in Arkansas.

DEVELOPMENT OF ORLANDO

1843	Aaron and Isaac Jernigan found Jernigan settlement.
1845	Florida becomes a state with 57,921 residents. Mosquito County changes its name to Orange County in an effort to lure settlers.
1857	Jernigan is renamed Orlando.
1870	'Orange fever' takes over and settlers begin planting citrus groves.
1875	Orlando is incorporated, becoming the seat of Orange County.

Walt Disney's plans for 'The Florida Project', which would become Walt Disney World

1880	Orlando's agricultural markets grow due to railroad extension.
1884	Fire destroys most of Orlando's downtown business district.
1887	The first African-American township in the US is built near Orlando.
1894–99	Severe frosts kill 95 percent of Orange County's citrus groves.
1898–9	Spanish-American War; Cuba wins independence from Spain.

20TH CENTURY

1903	First automobile is sold in Orlando; speed limit is 5mph (8kph).
1910–25	Land boom hits Florida. 'Tin can tourists' motor to Florida for winter.
1929	Mediterranean fruit flies devastate the citrus industry.
1936	Cypress Gardens opens south of Orlando.
1949	Gatorland opens.
1950s	Post-war automobile tourism skyrockets.
1957	The Glenn L. Martin Company of Baltimore (now Lockheed Martin) relocates to Orlando, starting a population boom.
1959	Busch Gardens opens in Tampa Bay.
1964–5	Walt Disney secretly buys 47 sq miles (122 sq km) of rural land and announces plans to build Walt Disney World in Orlando.
1971	The Magic Kingdom opens.
1973	SeaWorld Orlando opens.
1982	Epcot opens.
1989	Disney's Hollywood Studios opens (then Disney-MGM Studios).
1990	Universal Studios opens in Florida.
1998	Disney's Animal Kingdom opens.
1999	Islands of Adventure opens.

21ST CENTURY

2000	Discovery Cove opens.
2010	The Wizarding World of Harry Potter – Hogsmeade opens at Islands of Adventure.
2011	LEGOLAND Florida opens on former Cypress Gardens land.
2014	The Wizarding World of Harry Potter – Diagon Alley opens at Universal Orlando.
2016	50 people killed in shooting at Pulse, a gay nightclub.
2017	Volcano Bay water park opens at Universal Orlando; Pandora: The World of Avatar opens at Disney's Animal Kingdom.

BEST ROUTES

Familiar faces pose on the steps of Cinderella's Castle

THE MAGIC KINGDOM

This is the theme park that put Orlando on the map, and the one that most visitors head for first. All the classic Disneyland rides and characters are here, spread throughout the six lands of the Magic Kingdom, which encircle the towering spires of Cinderella Castle.

> **PARK SIZE:** 142 acres (57 hectares)
> **TIME:** One to two days
> **START/END:** Main Street, USA
> **POINTS TO NOTE:** Arrive early, especially if you only have one day here. Be at the gates at opening time and you'll be able to walk on to many rides with little or no wait.

As far back as 1959, Walt Disney began scouting for a location to build another theme park, one that would augment Disneyland in California and be more accessible to visitors in the eastern half of the country. In Orlando he found what he was looking for: warm weather, an inland location protected from hurricanes, the intersection of two major highways, and an airport. In fact, in 1965 he said, 'Here in Florida, we have something special we never enjoyed at Disneyland... the blessing of size. There's enough land here to hold all the ideas and plans we can possibly imagine.'

Disney began buying up land in secret, fearing that prices would skyrocket if word leaked out about his plans. He eventually acquired 47 sq miles (122 sq km) for his 'Florida Project', but it took years to transform the swamp and scrubland into a resort. Walt didn't live to see the realization of his dream. He died in 1966, five years before the Magic Kingdom, Disney's first Florida park, opened.

There's no one best way to tour the Magic Kingdom. The route you take will depend on whether you have children (and their ages), love thrill rides, are a first-time visitor, or have more than one day to spend. The best advice for everyone is to arrive early and head for the attraction you most want to see first (if you don't have a FastPass+ reservation for later – see page 32). There is only one entrance, which leads into Main Street, USA. From here, our route proceeds clockwise through the other five 'lands,' or themed areas, of the park. However, if you have young children you may want to start in Fantasyland, and if you have teenagers you'll probably head straight to the roller coasters in Frontierland or Tomorrowland – although Fantasyland has its own thriller now too. FastPass and FastPass+

Christmas is a magical time

times will also determine how you organize your day. Use the My Disney Experience mobile app to check up-to-date wait times for each attraction.

This route takes in the highlights of each area, but the park has many more shows and attractions besides. Some have different operating hours from the park, so pick up a *Times Guide* along with a park map at the entrance (or elsewhere around the park), and utilize the My Disney Experience app. You won't be able to see everything in one day, so use this route to help you prioritize the attractions most appealing to you.

Be sure to take a break at 3pm to watch the upbeat Disney Festival of Fantasy Parade. Then again, if you skip it, you'll find the rides a little bit emptier than usual. The park practically clears out once the parade ends.

MAIN STREET USA

The stroll down Main Street USA is great for setting the tone of the Magic Kingdom. The neat-as-a-pin storefronts, horse-drawn trolleys, and upbeat background music evoke a small Midwestern town of a century ago, and if it's a bit nostalgic it does the trick of taking you out of your stressed, modern mindset to a simpler place where Disney's imaginary world takes over.

Walt Disney World Railroad
You may want to hop aboard the steam-powered **Walt Disney World Railroad** ❶

Disney World ABCs

For information on the Magic Kingdom and all Disney World experiences, keep these numbers and websites handy:

Disney information: www.disneyworld.com

General park information: 407-824-4321 (automated) or 407-824-2222

Disney vacation packages: 407-939-7675, www.disneyworld.disney.go.com/plan/my-disney-experience/vacation-packages

Special events and tours: 407-WDW-TOUR (407-939-8687), www.disneyworld.disney.go.com/events-tours

Restaurant reservations: 407-WDW-DINE (407-939-3463), www.disneyworld.com/dining

Opening hours at Disney theme parks vary widely according to the season, the day of the week, and special events. They also differ from park to park. Always check the website, mobile app, or phone ahead when planning your visit. During super-busy seasons, smaller parks, especially the Magic Kingdom, occasionally fill up, so be sure to arrive early. Times for parades, shows, and night-time displays also change frequently. Each park prints a weekly *Times Guide* for these events. Guests staying at a WDW resort should ask about the Extra Magic Hours program, which gives early or extended admission to selected parks on certain days.

The original Pirates of the Caribbean ride

for a 20-minute ride around the park. It's a good way of seeing the various lands, or taking a quick route through the crowd to its other stops at Frontierland and Fantasyland. Otherwise, Main Street, USA is mostly lined with shops and eateries.

ADVENTURELAND

Like spokes on a wheel, paths lead out from the hub in front of the castle to the themed lands. Turn left and cross over the bridge to Adventureland, with

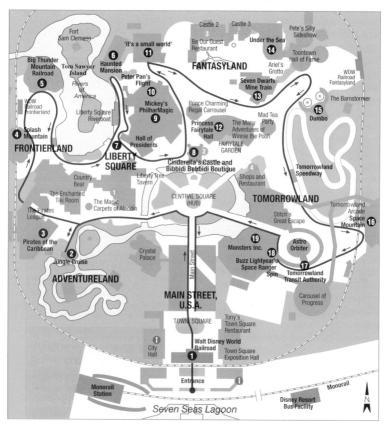

There are some gentler options   *Braving Splash Mountain*

its atmospheric, semi-tropical setting. Stop off for a bite at **Jungle Navigation Co. LTD. Skipper Canteen**, see ❶, if you're peckish early on.

Jungle Cruise

On your left, past the massive Swiss Family Treehouse, is the entrance to the **Jungle Cruise ❷**. This silly safari takes you down a tropical river past a delightful array of animatronic animals, from giraffes, lions, and zebras on the banks to a roaring hippo and a family of elephants bathing in the water. You'll also escape a head hunter or two and sail through a hidden temple. Despite the corny commentary from the captain, or because of it if you're keen for puns, it's an amusing ride, so jump on board early when the lines are still short.

Pirates of the Caribbean

From the number of youngsters sporting red-striped bandanas and pirate hats with dangling dreadlocks, it's not hard to guess that one of the most popular attractions is right next door. You'll board another boat for **Pirates of the Caribbean ❸**, this time for a swashbuckling sail through the booming cannons of a pirate raid on a small island town.

This ride into the rollicking world of a pirates' den is a Disney classic, each scene loaded with imaginative detail – watch for the drunken pigs joining in the celebrations. You'll also spot a familiar face among the remarkably lifelike pirates: Johnny Depp's Captain Jack

Sparrow. This attraction was in fact the inspiration for the blockbuster *Pirates of the Caribbean* movies, and the animatronic Depp was added later. The kids can get their buccaneer on at the nearby Pirate's League, offering swashbuckling adornments from temporary tattoos to full Captain Hook costumes.

FRONTIERLAND

Walk through the covered passage into Frontierland, which re-creates rustic settings from America's 19th-century frontier. Two of the park's best thrill rides are located here.

Splash Mountain

Splash Mountain ❹ starts off innocently enough as you ride a log flume past brightly colored scenes from *Song of the South*. Suddenly you emerge at the top of the mountain and plunge down into Brer Rabbit's Laughin' Place with a mighty splash. Those in the front and on the right are sure to get soaked, but it's a great way to cool off on a hot day.

Big Thunder Mountain Railroad

More thrills await at **Big Thunder Mountain Railroad ❺** across the way. The train cars whip around tight curves, through dark tunnels, and down into canyons beneath the mountain's red rock spires, said to be modeled after Bryce Canyon in Utah. This ride is exciting but not as terrifying as the big roller coasters, so it's a good option for more timid souls.

The eerily realistic Hall of Presidents

LIBERTY SQUARE

The Magic Kingdom's smallest land harks back to colonial times, with an old-fashioned riverboat and 18th-century architecture. Here is one of Disney's best-loved attractions, the **Haunted Mansion ❻**. The ghoulish fun is more clever than scary, full of creepy illusions, gallows humor, and animated apparitions, from the diners at a ghostly banquet to the ghost who hitches a ride in your doom buggy.

The Hall of Presidents

More in keeping with the theme of **Liberty Square ❼** is **The Hall of Presidents**. Even if you're not patriotic, the show is worth seeing for the authentic detail employed to create animatronic figures of all 45 American presidents, from their period dress to their mannerisms. You can almost believe America's long line of Chief Executives really has assembled on stage for this roll call.

FANTASYLAND

Continue around the back of **Cinderella Castle ❽** to Fantasyland, in many respects the essence of the Magic Kingdom. Due to a massive expansion (so big the area is often referred to as 'New Fantasyland'), this heart of the park is bigger than ever and filled with more to see and do. If you choose to stop and step inside the castle (and you should), exquisite mosaic murals recount the story of Cinderella along the main corridor walls. Also housed here is **Bibbidi Bobbidi Boutique** – if you're traveling with aspiring princes and princesses, let their once-in-a-lifetime wish come true with a complete transformation. For little girls, make-up, nails, accessories, and a new wardrobe (depending on the package you choose) will turn her into her favorite Disney heroine. Boys will become brave knights. You can also dine in the restaurant, **Cinderella's Royal Table,** see ❷.

Most of the attractions are based around Disney characters and geared for younger children, but adults are easily charmed by them too. Here you can unashamedly indulge your childhood fantasies.

Mickey's PhilharMagic

Not to be missed is **Mickey's PhilharMagic ❾**, arguably the best of the 30 shows in the Disney parks. The 150ft (50-meter) -wide screen is one of the largest of its kind ever made. Don your 3D glasses and enjoy all kinds of special effects popping literally right before your eyes, as Mickey and company make their own comical brand of musical magic.

Peter Pan's Flight

Next door, **Peter Pan's Flight ❿** is an enchanting ride over London by night to Neverland, with all the characters of this timeless tale. However, it has one of the slowest-moving lines in the park and much of the charm of this popular three-minute ride is lost after queuing for

Going underground on the Seven Dwarfs Mine Train

an hour or more. Get there early, or get a FastPass (see page 32).

'it's a small world'

Lines move more quickly down the road, as guests board small boats for a leisurely float around the globe in **'it's a small world'** ⓫. This audioanimatronic attraction was created for the 1964 World's Fair in New York, though it has since been refurbished and updated. It's still as delightful as ever, with dolls from around the world dressed in bright traditional costumes, dancing and singing the catchy theme tune in their own languages. The 10-minute ride is a good chance to cool off and escape from the rush outside.

Princess Fairytale Hall

Wander on past Prince Charming Regal Carrousel – a real one built by Italian carvers in 1917. Before you get to the slightly frightening The Many Adventures of Winnie the Pooh and the madly spinning teacups of the Mad Tea Party, you'll happen upon **Princess Fairytale Hall** ⓬. This air-conditioned gathering spot for autographs, photographs, and hugs has a regular line-up of headliner princesses.

Unless you have a reservation for a meal at **Be Our Guest**, see ❸, a spectacular French restaurant themed around *Beauty and the Beast*, stop in for a look at the magnificently adorned Beast's castle.

Seven Dwarfs Mine Train

The new **Seven Dwarfs Mine Train** ⓭ is a rickety roller coaster similar to Big Thun-

Tickets

There are many ticket options for visiting Walt Disney World (WDW) parks, and taking time to think them through is time – and money – well spent. You can buy a single-day ticket (currently $99 to $119 depending on whether you visit during value, regular or peak season), or get tickets for multiple days on a sliding scale; the cost per day drops the more days you purchase. You can then customize your ticket by adding various options: Park Hopper and Park Hopper Plus options allow unlimited visits to multiple parks for the length of your ticket and, in some cases, water park admission. If you have a MagicBand, a sort of electronic key/ID/credit card combo, you can buy a Memory Maker package to include digital photos of yourself. You can also use the Magic Your Way option to purchase packages that can cover hotel stays, meals, and snacks, as you wish. Tickets are non-transferable, and Disney enforces that strictly. You can buy tickets at the park entrances, online at www.disney world.com, on the mobile app, by phone (407-824-4321 or 407-934-7639), or by mail. Florida residents get discounted rates and those who visit often can benefit by buying an annual pass. Do not buy tickets from third parties unless they are authorized, such as Visit Orlando (www.visitorlando.com). People can and do get cheated.

Join Ariel and friends under the sea

der Mountain. Riders in the mine cars pivot back and forth while also climbing up and zooming down in a mine 'where a million diamonds shine'. At the end, you come to the dwarfs' cottage, with Snow White dancing inside.

Under the Sea – Journey of The Little Mermaid

Take a leisurely 5+-minute tour through an underground cavern with **Under the Sea ⑭** – you'll be tucked into a pastel clamshell car – to watch Ariel and her nautical friends experience major movie moments to the soundtrack highlights.

Dumbo, the Flying Elephant

Always a super-popular ride with an ultra-slow-moving line, the relocated and expanded **Dumbo, the Flying Elephant ⑮** brings a duo of rides – both involving tethered airplane-like little elephants riding above Storybook Circus, one going clockwise, the other counter-clockwise. The Circus itself entertains those waiting for their turn with interactive gadgets under a 'big top'. Bring tots onto **The Barnstomer Featuring the Great Goofini**, a starter roller-coaster with smallish dips.

TOMORROWLAND

The loud revving of race cars tells you that you've entered the land of the future. Speed freaks may be disappointed that the **Tomorrowland Indy Speedway 4D** is not really very fast, but kids love the chance to get behind the wheel.

Space Mountain

Most visitors head straight for **Space Mountain ⑯**, and for many this is a once-in-a-lifetime roller coaster. You ride up a 180ft (55-meter) mountain in the dark, through the blackness of outer space with only a few twinkling stars, and as your rocket car soars, dives, and whips round tight curves, it feels much faster than its top speed of 28mph (45kph).

Tomorrowland Transit Authority

Celebrate your return to earth at **Cosmic Ray's Starlight Café**, see ④, before taking

Beat the lines

On busy days, waits of 1–2 hours are not uncommon for popular attractions. Use Disney's FastPass and FastPass+ systems to make the most of your time. To use a FastPass, insert your park ticket into the machine located near the entrance to many rides. The machine will give you a time (usually an hour's window) when you can return and walk straight onto the ride without waiting in line. FastPass+ allows guests to reserve seats on an attraction up to 30 days beforehand (60 days if they'll be staying in a Disney World lodging facility). Make your plans online at www.mydisneyexperience.com or on the mobile app.

The park maps indicate which attractions have FastPass options. There are a limited number of FastPasses each day – so head for your favorite ride first unless you've pre-reserved with FastPass+.

Dumbo, the Flying Elephant

The park literally lights up at night

a calmer ride on the **Tomorrowland Transit Authority ⑰**. This gentle PeopleMover takes you round the land on an elevated track using a low-power, non-polluting motor. You can usually walk right on.

Buzz Lightyear Space Ranger

For more fun in the dark, ride into outer space on **Buzz Lightyear's Space Ranger Spin ⑱** to help the *Toy Story* hero save the toy universe from evil Emperor Zurg's robots. Fire your laser cannons, racking up points and setting off sight and sound effects.

Monsters, Inc. Laugh Floor

You can see Lilo & Co. in action at Stitch's Great Escape, which is only mildly entertaining, or have a planetary Dumbo-like experience on the Astro Orbiter. If you're pressed for time, though, make **Monsters, Inc. ⑲** a priority. This laugh-out-loud 400-seat show features one-eyed Mike Wazowski as the MC of a comedy show that, using technology, involves audience interaction.

NIGHT MAGIC

Stroll back down to Main Street, USA and find a good spot to take in Disney's night magic. First, *Once Upon a Time* features Mrs. Potts and Chip hosting a montage of cheerful Disney animated film scenes. Then, *Happily Ever After*, a dazzling fireworks spectacular with lasers and projected images, explodes most nights over Cinderella Castle.

Food and drink

① JUNGLE NAVIGATION CO. LTD. SKIPPER CANTEEN
Adventureland; $$
Explore the flavors of Africa, Asia, and South America at this Adventureland restaurant, themed around a jungle cruise.

② CINDERELLA'S ROYAL TABLE
Cinderella's Castle; $$$
Book well ahead to dine at this posh venue in the castle, where you'll meet Cinderella and her fellow princesses. The experiences include a photo-imaging package, and true princess fans can upgrade to yet more indulgent packages including a glass-slipper engagement.

③ BE OUR GUEST RESTAURANT
Beast's Castle; $$$
Dine in the Beast's ballroom, West Wing, or Rose Gallery at this grand restaurant, where contemporary French fare (with wine or beer at dinner) brings a turn of elegance within the Beast's sprawling, richly decorated castle. Lunches are less expensive and easier to access. Still no table? Go around the corner to Gaston's Tavern for grab-and-go snacks.

④ COSMIC RAY'S STARLIGHT CAFÉ
Tomorrowland; $
Probably the widest choice for a fast-food meal, from burgers and hot dogs to barbecue ribs and rotisserie chicken, served at three bays. There are healthy options too.

The monorail passing in front of Spaceship Earth

EPCOT

More than twice the size of the Magic Kingdom, Epcot is Walt Disney World Resort's least crowded theme park. It also has the most appeal for adults, with pavilions dedicated to technology, the land, and international destinations that educate as well as entertain.

PARK SIZE: 305 acres (123 hectares)
TIME: One to two days
START: Spaceship Earth
END: Canada Pavilion
POINTS TO NOTE: Try to spend two days here if you want to enjoy all the attractions in both sections of the park. The musical entertainment in World Showcase is excellent.

Walt Disney envisioned a planned residential community that would incorporate the exciting new ideas and technologies that were emerging in the 1960s. He called it the Environmental Prototype Community of Tomorrow. Several years after his death, his dream metamorphosed into EPCOT, Disney's second Orlando theme park, which opened in 1982. Epcot didn't turn out to be a real community but a theme park with a breed of educational twist; yet several years later the nearby town of Celebration – at first owned by the Disney folks, now independent – fulfilled parts of that vision.

Epcot has two very different sections: **Future World** and **World Showcase**. As with the Magic Kingdom, there's no best way to take it all in. It's a long way from one end of the park to the other, so two days will buy you the luxury of exploring at a leisurely pace. You don't necessarily need to devote each day to a separate section, but World Showcase in particular is meant for wandering and you don't want to find yourself dashing back for a FastPass in Future World from the far side of the lagoon. Live performers share cultural traditions at the pavilions at staggered times throughout the day, with the biggest concentration in the evening. Note that World Showcase opens a couple of hours later than Future World, normally at 11am, and stays open later in the evenings too.

Since Future World opens first, it's the logical place to begin. Your interests and the ages of your children will determine your route. Again, arrange for FastPass+ tickets in advance if you can, and/or head for your must-see attraction first. It's fairly easy to criss-cross this part of the park quickly, and the open spaces,

Expect fireworks at llumiNations: Reflections of Earth

fountains, and flowers are delightful. This route covers the park highlights.

FUTURE WORLD

More than 35 years have passed since its opening in 1982, and Epcot's world of the future has become the present. But periodic refurbishments have incorporated new technologies to keep it fresh and up-to-date. For example, Spaceship Earth used to show videocalls as a futuristic idea. Now that the technology is common – even on smartphones – the ride has evolved to be more futuristic. Riders tailor their own personal ending.

Spaceship Earth

As you enter the park, a gleaming sphere resembling a giant golf ball looms before you. This is **Spaceship Earth ❶**, Epcot's symbol. You may want to save this for later when the lines are shorter. Inside you board a time machine which transports you through the milestones of communication, with such lifelike scenes as a Greek scholar giving a maths lesson and Michelangelo painting the Sistine Chapel during the Renaissance. You even invent your own future world.

Innoventions

Just past Spaceship Earth you'll come to **Innoventions ❷**, a pavilion with interactive displays featuring new technology. In Colortopia, where three

Mission Space is the place to experience weightlessness

zones explore how color affects our lives, you can easily get carried away for an hour or two learning while having fun.

The Land

If you've chosen to save Spaceship Earth and Innoventions for later, head instead for **The Land ❸**, a prism-topped building home to Soarin', the park's most popular attraction. Certainly, if you don't have a FastPass+ reservation, proceed straight there: FastPasses go quickly and the day's allotment can be gone by noon.

Located on the lower floor, Soarin' is one of Disney's best rides. It simulates a hang-gliding flight over world highlights. Your seat rises 40 feet (12 meters) in the air with nothing but a seat belt between you and the surrounding high-definition, laser-projected screen. With the wind in your face and your feet dangling, you soar over six continents to see the Great Wall of China, Egypt's

The Seas with Nemo & Friends

pyramids, and Paris' Eiffel Tower; some sections have matching scents, such as roses as you view India.

In the meantime there's plenty to do nearby. Also in this building is Living with the Land, an educational boat ride through rainforest, desert, and prairie landscapes into the greenhouses of a plant research station, where new and innovative varieties of food crops are being cultivated that can help feed the world's growing population and benefit the planet.

The Seas with Nemo & Friends

Turn left out of The Land to visit **The Seas with Nemo & Friends ❹**. Here you can take a mild ride in a clamshell through Nemo's underwater world, with the cartoon characters superimposed into the real aquarium at the end.

You can while away hours in this pavilion watching the manatees, dolphins, sharks, and seahorses. The huge Caribbean Coral Reef – a 5.7 million gallon aquarium – holds real-life Nemos (clownfish) and over 60 species of sea creatures. There's also an entertaining interactive show, *Turtle Talk With Crush*.

Visit this pavilion early in the morning, if possible, when the fish in the Caribbean Coral Reef are usually fed. It's also fun to watch the manatees devouring heads of lettuce for their morning meal.

Universe of Energy

Continue round to **Universe of Energy ❺**, which houses *Ellen's Energy Adven-*

Discovering how cars are made and tested at Test Track

ture. The corny storyline takes comedienne Ellen DeGeneres back to prehistoric times, and while the dinosaurs are good and Bill Nye the Science Guy makes an appearance, the show could use some updating. Still, it is engaging and offers a 45-minute break from the heat.

Mission: SPACE

Hurry on to one of Epcot's most exciting attractions, **Mission: SPACE ❻**. Blast off to Mars in a simulator that re-creates the feeling of space flight, including the G-force, spinning and sense of weightlessness (and for some people, the motion sickness as well). Astronauts say it's amazingly close to the real experience. For those who don't feel up to chancing the full-on Orange version, there's a less intense Green alternative that eliminates the spinning and is just as much fun.

Test Track

For more vehicular thrills, **Test Track ❼** is right next door. This ride through an automobile proving ground is a must for anyone who loves cars and speed. You'll see and feel how acceleration, brakes, suspension, steering and other systems are rigorously tested as you zoom around the track at up to 65 mph (100 kph).

WORLD SHOWCASE

This section of the park is set around the **World Showcase Lagoon**, a circular body of water covering nearly 40 acres (16 hectares). It's about 1.3 miles (2 km) around, but the promenade is pleasantly broad and made for strolling. You can also take a water taxi across the lagoon, though this isn't a speedier option.

Each of the 11 pavilions represents a nation of the world, showcasing its landmarks, architecture, arts, food, drink and, of course, its wares. You'll often find Disney characters from animated movies tied to the locale, such as Mulan in China or Jasmine and Aladdin in Morocco. Some of the pavilions also have rides, films and cultural exhibits in addition to shops and restaurants. Shops sometimes feature visiting artists demonstrating crafts from their homeland.

Supplementary tours

Disney World offers many fee-based behind-the-scenes tours, and Epcot's are among the best. Some are available year-round, others only during special events. Behind the Seeds provides a closer look at the hydroponic gardens and fish farm in The Land. Epcot Seas Adventures – Aqua Tour invites adventurers to snorkel with more than 6,000 sea creatures in their underwater world. With DiveQuest, scuba enthusiasts swim with the sharks and other aquarium dwellers. Dolphins in Depth teaches participants about dolphin behavior. For information on these and other tours, call 407-WDW-TOUR (407-939-8687), or visit the website at www.disneyworld.com/tours.

Frozen Ever After is Norway's star attraction

Most pavilions have performances periodically throughout the day and into the evening, listed in the park's *Times Guide* and on the My Disney Experience mobile app. Among the highlights are China's Jeweled Dragon Acrobats and the Mariachi Cobre band (Mexico).

World Showcase is home to some of the best food in the entire resort, so this is the place to indulge. Spirits-driven travelers come here to 'drink their way around the world' at assorted geographically tied bars and kiosks. Even the 'casting' is authentic – many of the employees in the pavilions at World Showcase are natives of the country they represent.

Best of all are the pavilions themselves. Each is an impressively detailed rendition of the landmarks, buildings,

Pizza at Via Napoli in the Italy pavilion

squares, and other elements that represent a country's culture and history. You can spend hours here just leisurely browsing and admiring the artful features you see.

Mexico, Norway, and China

This route proceeds clockwise around the lagoon, beginning with **Mexico** ❽. Inside the striking Aztec pyramid are a colorful array of shops and intriguing cultural exhibits set around a Mexican-style plaza. You can take a labyrinthine boat ride with *The Three Caballeros*, which floats by the romantic San Angel Inn restaurant. La Cava del Tequila has more than one hundred varieties of its namesake beverage.

A Viking longboat and a beautiful wooden stave church are highlights of the town square in **Norway** ❾. Frozen Ever After, a mild thrill ride themed to the animated movie *Frozen*, is the main attraction. It includes popular songs, and delights fans of Arendelle with glimpses of trolls as well as Anna and Elsa. The resplendent restaurant Akershus Royal Banquet Hall hosts princess character meals all day long.

With its circular temple, landscaped gardens and soft, traditional music, **China** ❿ is an oasis of tranquillity. *Reflections of China*, a Circle-Vision 360 film, completely surrounds you with images from this truly beautiful ancient land. Yet more fascinating are replicas of the famous Terra Cotta warriors. Chinese acrobats perform in the plaza regularly

Italy's emphasis is on food

Moroccan flavors sing at Spice Road Table

and the shopping at this pavilion is dazzling and diverse.

Germany and Italy

The main attraction in **Germany ⑪** is the **Biergarten restaurant**, see ①, a buffet with live oompah-enthusiastic entertainment (see page 40). Shops are set around a statue of St George in the half-timbered square.

An amazing re-creation of St. Mark's Square in Venice, with exquisite architectural detail in everything from the Doge's Palace to the statues, makes **Italy ⑫** one of the finest pavilions here, although one of the most boring, since it has no attraction. The Italian shops are secondary to the scenery, but the Italian fare in the two restaurants by New York's Patina Group is good – try **Via Napoli Ristorante e Pizzeria**, see ②.

The American Adventure

Be ready for a big dollop of patriotism at **The American Adventure ⑬**, where *The American Adventure* show does an admirable job of covering highlights in American history in 26 minutes with a cast of superb audio-animatronic characters led by Ben Franklin and Mark Twain. The America Gardens Theatre hosts outdoor concerts regularly, and the Voices of Liberty, a cappella group, sing patriotic songs inside the main building.

Japan, Morocco, and France

Japan ⑭ is another tranquil spot, with beautifully landscaped grounds, a pagoda, and striking Japanese architecture. The Bijutsu-Kan Gallery houses cultural exhibits and the Japanese drumming shows called Matsuriza are spirited. The mini Mitsukoshi department store will satisfy your souvenir needs with gift items from elegant chopsticks and tea sets to pearls extracted from oysters you select.

Beautiful handmade mosaic tiles were used to construct the fine replicas of the Koutoubia Minaret and Bab Boujouloud arched gate in **Morocco ⑮**. Behind is a winding souk where you can get authentic wares from carpets to henna tattoos. Guided tours of the pavilion highlight the country's culture and history. Check out the handcrafted objects d'art behind the stained-glass doors of the Gallery of Arts and History. The Tangierine Café offers

---

Nightly extravaganza

After dark, don't miss Epcot's night-time extravaganza, *IllumiNations – Reflections of Earth*. The 12-minute show is a mixture of fireworks, lasers, colors, fountains, and lights, set to music and centered on an enormous globe in the middle of the lagoon. It's visible from all around the promenade – anywhere where you can see both the water and the sky – but stake your spot at least 30 minutes in advance. Good viewing points include Showcase Plaza (at the bridge with Future World) and the Rose & Crown Pub in the United Kingdom.

Typically French fare on offer in France's pavilion

quick and tasty Moroccan dishes; Spice Road Table, see page 113, serves more exotic Moroccan cuisine in large and small plates; while the fancier Restaurant Marrakesh specializes in Americanized versions of Moroccan classics with entertainment by belly dancers.

If you've been to Paris, you'll enjoy the **France** ⑯ pavilion's pastiche of this great city, from the Eiffel Tower to the Belle Epoque architecture. And of course, it has two of Epcot's best restaurants (including **Monsieur Paul**, see ❸), plus a patisserie and a rather addictive gelato shop, L'Artisan des Glaces. *Impressions de France*, a fine film narrated by a Frenchman with a smoky voice, takes you on a tour of the French countryside set to stirring music by French composers.

United Kingdom and Canada

Cross the replica Pont des Arts to the **United Kingdom** ⑰, where the country's history is represented by a thatched cottage, a castle, a Georgian square, Tudor chimneys, and half-timbered and Victorian buildings. There's even a pair of the traditional red phone boxes that are a rarity in Britain itself these days. Naturally, the main attractions are the **Rose & Crown Pub**, see ❹, and the fish and chip counter, although the stores' tea sets and family crests make for great retail therapy. A band that plays Beatles tunes is often on the schedule.

An imposing totem pole marks the entrance to **Canada** ⑱, alongside a trading post and a Rocky Mountain waterfall with the Hôtel du Canada rising up behind. The Circle-Vision 360 film *O Canada!*, narrated by Martin Short, is a look at the wildlife, people, cities, and landscapes of this vast and varied nation.

Food and drink

❶ BIERGARTEN RESTAURANT
Germany Pavilion; $$

This buffet-style restaurant, set in a dimly lit mock-timber house, serves *bratwurst* and an array of German fare. The healthy selection of beers will get you in the mood for the live Bavarian music.

❷ VIA NAPOLI RISTORANTE E PIZZERIA
Italy Pavilion; $$

A bustling family restaurant specializing in authentic Neapolitan pizza.

❸ MONSIEUR PAUL
France Pavilion; $$$$

Exquisitely prepared French cuisine in a light, bright, fine-dining setting, all a tribute to renowned chef Paul Bocuse.

❹ ROSE & CROWN PUB AND DINING ROOM
United Kingdom Pavilion; $–$$

Bass ale, Guinness stout, and traditional pub grub – fish and chips, meat pies, ploughman's lunches, and even sticky toffee pudding – ensure this popular watering hole is busy throughout the day. Try for a waterside table.

Palm-lined Sunset Boulevard

DISNEY'S HOLLYWOOD STUDIOS

Hollywood helped make Walt Disney famous, and this theme park celebrates the magic of the movies. From a 3D living arcade game to a dazzling night-time extravaganza, Mickey pulls a whole lot of enchantment out of his sorcerer's hat.

> **PARK SIZE:** 135 acres (54 hectares)
> **TIME:** One day
> **START:** Hollywood Boulevard
> **END:** Hollywood Hills Amphitheater
> **POINTS TO NOTE:** Get here at least 30 minutes in advance (more on busy days) to claim a good seat for the stunt shows and *Fantasmic!*

Disney's third Florida theme park made its debut in May 1989 as Disney-MGM Studios, after a neck-and-neck race with Universal Studios to open first (Disney won by a hair). Both companies had been simultaneously developing plans for a movie-themed park for a great number of years, but they have evolved into very different creatures, each with their own unforgettable attractions.

In January 2008, the park changed its name to Disney's Hollywood Studios. With neon-lit Art-Deco movie palaces lining Sunset Boulevard, it reflects Tinseltown's heyday of the 1930s and '40s.

It's no shocker that Disney devotes an entire park to film. Walt Disney earned more Academy Award Oscars than any other person in motion-picture history. He was nominated 63 times for work ranging from animation to documentaries and live-action short subjects, and won 26 awards, beginning with an Honorary Oscar for the creation of Mickey Mouse in 1931. In 1941 he received the Irving G. Thalberg Memorial Award, given to creative producers responsible for consistently high-quality motion-picture production – considered to be the industry's highest accolade.

Currently with fewer must-see attractions than the other Disney parks, this one can easily be toured in a day, although that might change when the immersive Star Wars land opens in 2019 and the Toy Story area expands to incorporate more elements. And with park areas less defined, you will spend a fair amount of time navigating back and forth to hit the show times. Shows are a big part of Disney's Hollywood Studios, and their schedules will largely determine your route. It's a good idea to spend a few minutes with a *Times Guide* or the My Disney Experience app when you enter the

Indiana Jones Epic Stunt Spectacular!

park to work out which shows you want to see, and plan your day around them.

The park's thrill rides, stunt show, and kiddie programs are scattered. This route proceeds in a roughly clockwise direction around the park, to end at the Hollywood Hills ampitheater for a fabulous finale.

LIGHTS, CAMERA, ACTION

Walk up **Hollywood Boulevard** towards the big plaza – and center of the park – which often has shows going on. The walk itself will be entertaining as classic movie characters drive and walk among visitors – this colorful troupe is the Citizens of Hollywood Cavalcade of Stars. **Center Stage** ❶ is used for seemingly impromptu productions several times a day.

Turn left and walk toward Echo Lake. Note that on the opposite side of the lake is a great lunch spot to return to later, the **50s Prime Time Café**, see ❶, or instead try **The Hollywood Brown Derby** on Hollywood Boulevard,

see ❷. For now, carry on to **For the First Time in Forever: A Frozen Sing-Along Celebration** ❷, a wonderful 30-minute show inside the Hyperion Theater that's

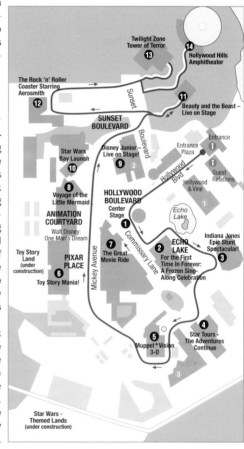

Star Wars Launch Bay

Identifying targets on Toy Story Mania!

a condensed tribute to the popular animated movie.

Carry on to the **Indiana Jones Epic Stunt Spectacular! ❸**. This exciting show re-creates action scenes from the popular Indiana Jones movies, and afterwards demonstrates how the furious fights and great escapes are achieved. If you've always wondered what it would be like to be a movie 'extra', you may get your chance. A few audience members are chosen at random, and after going backstage for costumes and rehearsal, they turn up onstage during the show. Get there early and sit near the front to increase your chances.

Further on is **Star Tours – The Adventures Continue ❹**, an updated version of a long-running favorite based on the Star Wars movies. The 3D experience is different every time. After booking a flight with the familiar robots R2-D2 and C-3PO, you board a spacecraft for what becomes a wild intergalactic ride. The flight simulator pitches and tilts as it dodges laser blasts and other hazards, creating a turbulently realistic and thrilling ride.

Proceed next toward Muppet Courtyard. If hungry bellies need filling, **Mama Melrose's Ristorane Italiano**, see ❸, will do the trick. Otherwise, behind the whimsical Miss Piggy fountain is the continuously running show, **Muppet*Vision 3-D ❺**. This entertaining production with the Muppet characters mixes 3-D film and audio-animatronics with all kinds of special effects. Just watch out for the cream pies!

THE BIG BUZZ

Behind Commissary Lane is an entire land called **Pixar Place,** which is dedicated to the characters of the Toy Story movies, including Buzz and Woody. The highlight – and possibly the park's hardest-to-get seat – is **Toy Story Mania! ❻**. (Sign up with FastPass+ if possible.) After weaving through a waiting area lined with oversized replicas of childhood toys and games, you'll ride a two-seat tram while hitting targets for points in a 4D carnival-style game. It's like Magic Kingdom's Buzz Lightyear ride, only more eye-popping because it's newer and higher-tech. Behind a construction wall, a major expansion is underway: Andy's backyard will be the backdrop for Toy Story Land, an 11-acre (4.5-hectare) world with a Slinky Dog-themed family roller coaster and a spin ride based on the Aliens.

MOVIE HEAVEN

At the back of the main plaza is a replica of one of Hollywood's most famous landmarks, Mann's Chinese Theatre, which contains **The Great Movie Ride ❼**. This attraction is an adult's delight. Cinematic memories are evoked with classic film clips and lifesize acted scenes from *Mary Poppins*, *Casablanca*, *Tarzan*, *Alien*, and many more. A highlight is the Munchkinland scene from *The Wizard of Oz*, with a scary appearance by the Wicked Witch of the West. Behind the theater is Walt Disney: One Man's Dream, a museum with

The Rock 'n' Roller Coaster has a giant red Fender Stratocaster at its entrance

artifacts related to the man who started it all.

Continue to Animation Courtyard. Young families will be interested in the area's kiddie fun: the **Voyage of the Little Mermaid 8**, a show with a live Ariel; and **Disney Junior – Live on Stage! 9**, featuring popular characters from the Mickey Mouse Clubhouse.

At the **Star Wars Bay Launch 10**, fans of the science-fiction series can view pertinent artifacts, tour memorabilia galleries, and play interactive video games. (At night, visitors can watch the outdoor *Star Wars: A Galactic Spectacular*, a show with projections onto the Chinese Theatre.)

Take a stroll down Sunset Boulevard; with its Art-Deco movie palaces, it's one of the most atmospheric streets in the park. On the right is the Theater of the Stars, where **Beauty and the Beast – Live on Stage 11**, a musical show, is performed several times a day. It's well worth seeing this colorful production, and the singing-dancing teapot, clock, and candlestick are especially delightful.

At the end of the street, you'll find the park's two biggest thrill rides. **The Rock 'n' Roller Coaster Starring Aerosmith 12** races from 0 to 60mph (100kph) in 2.8 seconds. Your stretch limo carries on to the party through loops and corkscrew turns, while blasting the band's rock hits. Essentially across the street, the Hollywood Tower Hotel is home to the **Twilight Zone Tower of Terror 13**. Inside you'll take an elevator ride through eerie scenes reminiscent of the classic TV series. Amid random drops the ride culminates in a 13-story plunge from the top of the tower.

Another path leads to the **Hollywood Hills Amphitheater 14**. This is the setting for the night-time show *Fantasmic!*. From atop a mountain in the middle of the lake, Mickey conjures up an extravaganza of lasers, lights, dancing fountains, fireworks, a menacing dragon, king cobra, and a shipful of Disney characters.

Food and drink

1 50S PRIME TIME CAFÉ
Echo Lake; $–$$
At this reincarnation of mom's kitchen, waiters discipline parents who do not clean their plates, or are caught with elbows on the table. The food is just what you'd expect from mom too: meatloaf, peas, pot roast, fried chicken, and indulgent desserts, but modernized for contemporary tastes.

2 THE HOLLYWOOD BROWN DERBY
Hollywood Boulevard; $$$
If you have the budget, reserve a table at this recreation of a Los Angeles classic, where the Cobb Salad was invented and is still served.

3 MAMA MELROSE'S RISTORANTE ITALIANO
Muppet Courtyard; $$
Red-sauce Italian favorites plus especially good flatbreads in a homey setting.

Giraffes are a likely sighting in the Africa zone

ANIMAL KINGDOM

Real animals take center stage at Disney World's fourth theme park. Go on a safari through the African plains, explore a jungle trail, and take in the most colorful shows. There's a couple of thrill rides and a menagerie of Disney characters thrown in. And then there's Pandora: The World of Avatar, the kingdom's sparkling new attraction.

PARK SIZE: 403 acres (163 hectares)
TIME: One to two days
START: Oasis
END: Discovery Island
POINT TO NOTE: You can see all the animal highlights here in a day; two days is needed to take it at a leisurely pace and explore 12-acre (5-hectare) Pandora: The World of Avatar too.

Animal Kingdom is different from the other Disney theme parks. Opened in 1998, its focus is on animal conservation and letting visitors experience the wonder of the creatures who share our planet. Walt Disney himself was a keen proponent of conservation back in the 1940s and 1950s and won several Academy Awards for his documentaries on the natural world.

At more than 400 acres (1.6 sq km), Animal Kingdom is the largest of the Disney World parks, but most of the land is devoted to naturalistic habitat for the animals. About 2,000 animals (300 species) live in seemingly open and impressively landscaped surroundings, giving visitors a sense of exploration as they search for the inhabitants along well-blended trails and paths. Most animals have space to roam (and space to hide), and nowhere does it feel like a zoo. Animal welfare is paramount at Animal Kingdom. The park generally closes earlier than the other parks in the resort, and even on late nights the animals are brought in at their regular time to avoid stress. The new Pandora land and *Rivers of Light* show extend stays into the evening hours.

The hub of the park is Discovery Island. Its centerpiece is the enormous Tree of Life, the park's icon. From here bridges lead across the Discovery River to the other five themed sections of the park.

Unless you have a FastPass+ reservation, head for the Kilimanjaro Safari first: lines are shorter and the animals generally more active in the morning than in the heat of the day. Or, if thrill rides are your thing, make your way to Asia for a chance to ride Expedition Everest. Tickets for the new Pandora rides are also ultra-hot.

The Tree of Life, Animal Kingdom's centerpiece

Pick up the *Times Guide* along with the park map at the entrance, and check the show times. There are fewer shows here than at the other parks, but *Flights of Wonder*, *Finding Nemo – The Musical*, and *Festival of the Lion King* are all unmissable attractions. It's worth planning your day to fit them all in. Go out of your way to experience the night-time show, *Rivers of Light*. With live performances, high-tech projections, and spirited music, it is truly spectacular. FastPass+ and dining packages with premium seating are available at www.mydisneyexperience.com and the My Disney Experience smartphone app.

This route proceeds clockwise around the park through the six lands, noting the top attractions.

OASIS

Shortly after the entrance gates you enter this small and gentle land. Just like on a real safari, guests often rush through here in pursuit of bigger game. But the **Oasis Exhibits ❶** repay those who linger with a collection of fascinating animals including warthogs, giant anteater, wallabies, and Hyacinth macaw. The calming landscape of lush foliage, pools, and waterfalls helps you change gear, ready for the natural world that lies ahead.

DISCOVERY ISLAND

Cross the bridge to Discovery Island. It may not be nature's handiwork, but the 14-story **Tree of Life ❷** is a wonder to behold. Disney artists took more than a year to create this artificial banyan tree, carving some 325 birds, bugs, mammals, and reptiles into its trunk and 8,000 branches. See how many you can spot along the Discovery Island trails that wind around its base.

Also here is the entertaining 3-D movie, **It's Tough to be a Bug! ❸**. Most adults and older kids love it, but the sounds, smells, and other special effects can be quite startling and may upset young children or those with a strong aversion to creepy-crawlies.

Tiffins, see ❶, a full-service restaurant with flavors from around the world, is an excellent place to fuel up and reboot. Its adjacent Nomad Lounge has light bites, cocktails and water views.

PANDORA – THE WORLD OF AVATAR

Themed around the movie *Avatar*, this high-tech 12-acre (5-hectare) land, which debuted in May 2017, astounds science-fiction fans with intensely hued floating mountains and bioluminescent flora. You'll feel like you're flying aboard a winged banshee on **AVATAR Flight of Passage ❹**. Or take to the water on the **Na'vi River Journey ❺** through a glowing rainforest, a gentler ride that's great for families. If you want to stay immersed in all things Avatar, visit the themed **Satu'li Canteen**, see ❷.

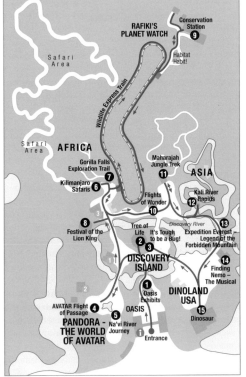

Zebra in Africa   *Exploring Avatar on the Na'vi River Journey*

AFRICA

Cross back to Discovery Island and continue on into Africa. Here the Animal Kingdom comes into its own. At **Kilimanjaro Safaris** ❻ you take a realistically bumpy ride in an open-air safari vehicle out into landscape reminiscent of an African savannah. The animals roam freely, but you're fairly certain to see elephants, giraffe, zebra, and various breeds of antelope. Lions, black rhino, white rhino and hippos may be more elusive. (The behind-the-scenes Wild Africa Trek (charge) gets you even closer to the animals and includes thrills and lunch. It's pricey but worth it. Reserve online or on the My Disney Experience app.)

The fascinating journey includes a chase after so-called ivory poachers, but this element of the storyline has been played down in recent years. Drivers point out animals as they come into sight. As animals – and thus safaris – are always unpredictable, you will see different things at different times of day, so consider riding twice if time allows. Generally, more animals will be active in early morning and late evening than in the midday heat.

After all that bouncing around you'll be glad to put your feet on solid ground and wander the **Gorilla Falls Exploration Trail** ❼ at your own pace. As you might expect, gorillas are the highlight here, though when it's hot they

All aboard the Wildlife Express Train

may spend much of the day curled up in the shade in the dense vegetation. Another treat is the underwater hippo viewing area, where it's fascinating to see these great beasts taking a swim.

Africa is also where you'll find the Harambe Theatre and its **Festival of the Lion King** ❽, an upbeat show with vibrant costumes and infectious music. You'll find yourself clapping along. Just opposite, the **Tusker House restaurant**, see ❸, houses a buffet with character meals and an exceptional variety of vegetarian and vegan offerings.

RAFIKI'S PLANET WATCH

Board the **Wildlife Express Train** for the short ride to this separate area of the park, with a peek at some of the

The Wild Africa Trek takes you behind the scenes

behind-the-scenes animal enclosures on the way. The main attraction here is the **Conservation Station** ❾, with interactive exhibits on wildlife and habitats, veterinary care and research, designed to encourage conservation awareness. This area is dull except to the most education-minded, so make it a low priority if you're in a hurry.

Return by train to the station, then make your way to the river's shore and turn left.

ASIA

As Africa gives way to Asia, duck into the open-air theater for **Flights of Wonder** ❿, a show where a variety of birds demonstrate their intelligence and aerial prowess. Feathered performers range from a grape-snatching hornbill to a swooping crowned crane to hawks, eagles, owls, and macaws.

Discover Komodo dragons and other exotic Asian creatures on the **Maharajah Jungle Trek** ⓫. Wander at your own pace through a Southeast Asia rainforest setting. Bengal tigers lounge against the walls of an ancient ruined palace or come right up to inspect you through the glass as if you were the specimen they've come to see. There's no barrier, however, between you and the giant fruit bats hanging round the corner, lazily stretching their 6ft (2-meter) wingspans.

Asia is also the site of two thrill rides. **Kali River Rapids** ⓬ is a sure way to

The Kali River Rapids

Expedition Everest roller coaster

cool off as you ride the white-water raft through an endangered rainforest, literally soaking up the adventure. Looming above the eastern side of the park is the snow-capped peak of **Expedition Everest – Legend of the Forbidden Mountain ⑬**, which until Pandora opened was Animal Kingdom's most coveted thrill ride. Board the train for a high-speed roller-coaster adventure down rugged slopes into the land of the Yeti.

DINOLAND USA

A prehistoric theme takes over across the bridge in Dinoland USA. The Theater in the Wild is home to the fabulous stage show **Finding Nemo – The Musical ⑭**. Live actors wielding character puppets (the jellyfish are positively enchanting) and a charming story set to an original musical score make this an unforgettable production.

Much of this land has a carnival park feel, with kiddie rides and midway games. Younger children enjoy digging in the Boneyard. The biggest thrill here for anyone over 10 is **Dinosaur ⑮**, a scary dark ride that takes you back in time to rescue DNA from the last iguanodon. You'll encounter some moving, breathing, fiercely realistic dinosaurs on this jarring prehistoric time trip.

Stroll back across the bridge to Discovery Island, and end your visit in more tranquil surroundings beneath the Tree of Life.

Food and drink

① TIFFINS

Discovery Island; $$$

Before building Animal Kingdom, Disney's Imagineers traveled through Asia and Africa to gather ideas. Mementos of their travels decorate this table-service restaurant, where global flavors create one of the best theme-park meals at Disney World. The adjacent Nomad Lounge is ideal for a grown-up break from sightseeing.

② SATU'LI CANTEEN

Pandora – The World of Avatar; $

Extend your stay in this exciting new land by having a quick-service meal at Satu'li Canteen (you can pre-order on your Disney app). Hand-woven tapestries and Pandoran cooking tools set the tone for the eatery's 'pods', which are bao-style sandwiches, plus familiar and exotic foods like wood-grilled chicken or chili-spiced tofu.

③ TUSKER HOUSE

Africa; $$

A good all-you-can-eat buffet of carved meats, salads, and desserts – with a tremendous bounty for vegetarians – is served inside at lovely carved tables or outdoors under a thatched roof. Donald Duck, in safari attire, and other characters come by to visit during breakfast, lunch, and dinner, so reserve your spot early.

The entrance to Universal Orlando Resort

UNIVERSAL STUDIOS FLORIDA

Amid the thrill rides, cartoon characters, shows, and attractions, you may come across the next hit movie being made, for Universal Studios is a working film studio as well as a theme park.

PARK SIZE: 108 acres (44 hectares)
TIME: One day
START: Production Central
END: Hollywood
POINTS TO NOTE: With careful planning, in a long day you can hit most of the highlights here and also take in some of the rides at Islands of Adventure. But if you want to catch all the shows, it's best to allow two days here.

Universal Studios Florida is a theme park for everyone who loves movies. While the rides and attractions feature plenty of popular film characters, it is not as character-led as the Disney parks and has a very different, earthier feel. Facades here look like authentic back-lots. The fact that the film studios here opened in 1988, two years before the theme park, gives it added authenticity.

That said, when it comes to fun and entertainment, Universal Studios puts on a star performance. More than twice the size of its California counterpart, it is a popular park that, along with its sister,

Islands of Adventure, has some seriously scary thrill rides. The pair, together with the 30-acre (12-hectare) CityWalk dining and nightlife complex (see page 56) in between, plus the Volcano Bay water park and several hotels, make up Universal Orlando Resort. One of the two theme parks will gain a Nintendo-themed area in coming years, but details have not yet been announced. If possible, allow one full day for Universal Studios and a second for Islands of Adventure. If budget allows, buy an Express Pass that allows you to skip the lines – it's free if you're staying at an on-site hotel. Single riders can also move through the lines more quickly by taking up spare seats in roller-coaster cars and on other rides. Universal offers a variety of single-day and multi-day passes to one or both parks, plus the new Volcano Bay water park. Per-day prices decrease when you buy larger multiday packs.

It's easy to get around the park, so your interests and show times will largely determine your route. Other than Harry Potter and the Escape from Gringotts within The Wizarding World of Harry

Partying with the Blues Brothers on Delancey Street

Potter – Diagon Alley, whose popularity is without peer, the most in-demand rides tend to be the newest. Other stars include Men in Black: Alien Attack, Revenge of the Mummy, and Shrek 4-D; on busy days, head for these first. This route describes the highlights of many shows and attractions, proceeding in a clockwise direction from the entrance. In 2018, Fast & Furious: Supercharged

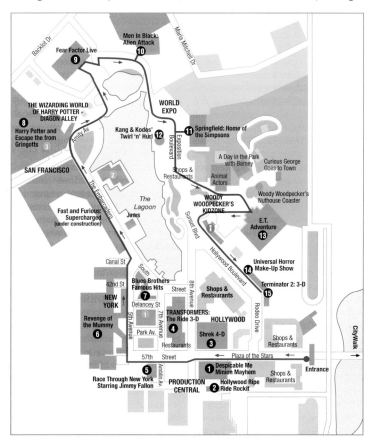

Experience New York from a different angle

is due to open, based on Universal Pictures' highest-grossing film franchise.

Use the Universal Orlando Resort app to help you buy tickets, get around, see wait times, and plan around shows.

PRODUCTION CENTRAL

From the entrance gate walk up Plaza of the Stars. On your left is Production Central with **Despicable Me Minion Mayhem ❶** and **Hollywood Rip Ride Rockit ❷**. The newest of these, Despicable Me, will have the whole family laughing. Over the road is **Shrek 4-D ❸**, a delightful movie in which special effects let you join the gentle ogre and Princess Fiona on their ill-fated honeymoon. **TRANSFORMERS: The Ride 3-D ❹** is found to the right of these.

NEW YORK

Walk up 57th Street into New York, a backlot with some marvelous facades of the Big Apple. The newest addition to the area is **Race Through New York Starring Jimmy Fallon ❺**, a simulator ride that makes you feel like you're flying through the glittering city.

Another highlight is **Revenge of the Mummy ❻**, a thrill-filled coaster that pits you against the Mummy who is after your soul. You'll plunge into a tomb of darkness, through balls of fire and past fearsome warriors from the dead.

Nearby on Delancey Street, Jake and Elwood strut their stuff across from Irish pub **Finnegan's Bar and Grill**, see ❶, in a rockin' show featuring renditions of **The Blues Brothers ❼** famous hits.

SAN FRANCISCO

Walk on into San Francisco along the Embarcadero. Notice the turntable in the middle of the cobbled street, just like the ones used to turn the cable cars in the real city. There are some lovely views across the lake by **Lombard's Seafood Grille**, see ❷. The major attraction here will debut in 2018 – Fast & Furious: Supercharged – where high-speed cars will provide the backdrop for high-octane thrills.

THE WIZARDING WORLD OF HARRY POTTER – DIAGON ALLEY

When The Wizarding World of Harry Potter opened at Islands of Adventure in 2014, it ushered in a gush of tourism for the park, which later built the Harry Potter mini-park here, themed as Diagon Alley; the two are connected by a train called *The Hogwarts Express*. Whether you just want to take in the otherworldly British universe, enjoy a drink at the **Leaky Cauldron**, see ❸, or are game for a full-on thrill ride, you will feel as if you are part of Harry Potter's world.

Harry Potter and the Escape from Gringotts ❽ is the headliner here. As you ride through the tunnels below Gringotts bank, you'll encounter dangers from the villainous Voldemort and troublesome trolls. 3D touches bring extra

The Simpsons Ride   *TRANSFORMERS: The Ride 3-D*

life to an already big thrill. Find time for Diagon Alley's gift shops, where interactive wands, wizardly robes, and Quidditch equipment make great souvenirs.

WORLD EXPO

Continue on to World Expo, where you'll find **Fear Factor Live 9**, a reality show in which audience participants are chosen in advance. If you have the nerve for it, turn up for casting in front of the stadium about 75 minutes before the show. **Men in Black: Alien Attack 10** is also here. It's tremendous fun as you ride a spinning car through a darkened city, zapping aliens with your laser gun and racking up points to get your black suit.

SPRINGFIELD: HOME OF THE SIMPSONS

On **The Simpsons Ride 11**, you'll join Homer and family on a wild ride through Krusty the Clown's fantasy amusement park, which includes thrill rides, dark rides, and entertainment. You can also brave the frightfully named **Kang & Kodos' Twirl 'n' Hurl 12**, which involves trying to zap Springfield characters with lasers while spinning around them.

WOODY WOODPECKER'S KIDZONE

This section of the park is filled with diversions for younger visitors, from sing-alongs with Barney to animal shows to playgrounds. A highlight for adults is

the **E.T. Adventure 13**, a charming bicycle ride through the night sky to take E.T. back to his very colorful but ailing planet.

HOLLYWOOD

Sunset Boulevard brings you to the heart of Hollywood, where more tricks of the trade are revealed in the **Universal Horror Make-Up Show 14**. It's humorous as well as gruesome. Further down Hollywood Boulevard, **Terminator 2: 3-D 15** uses the original actors in a 3-D film with special effects and live action to continue the story where the movies left off.

Food and drink

1 FINNEGAN'S BAR AND GRILL
Delancey Street, New York; tel: 407-224-3613; $$
Burgers, chicken, seafood, corned beef, and Irish stew are on the menu, and there's a daily happy hour.

2 LOMBARD'S SEAFOOD GRILLE
San Francisco; tel: 407-224-3613; $$
This lakeside restaurant serves great clam chowder and seafood dishes, and tasty pastas as well.

3 LEAKY CAULDRON
Wizarding World; tel: 407-224-3613; $$
Counter-service pub featuring British staples plus colorful beverages adapted from the pages of the Harry Potter books.

The Incredible Hulk Coaster

ISLAND OF ADVENTURE

From comic-book heroes to a boy with magical powers, fantasy worlds collide to make a theme park that delights all ages. Among its whimsical backdrops, drenching raft trips, and exciting thrill rides – not to mention Harry Potter's Hogsmeade – you'll find some of Orlando's most terrifying roller coasters and its most awesome 3-D adventure.

PARK SIZE: 101 acres (41 hectares)
TIME: One day
START: Port of Entry
END: Seuss Landing
POINTS TO NOTE: Try to get to your top outdoor attractions first, especially in summer when there are often thunderstorms in the afternoon. Park rides will close if lightning is within 5 miles (8km).

Volcano Bay

Opened in 2017, Volcano Bay is Universal's newest venture, a huge water park neighboring Islands of Adventure. You'll still have thrills, relax, and cool off as you wish, but new technology means you won't need to wait on lines or haul huge rubber tubes uphill yourself. Themed as Waturi, a remote fictional Pacific island, the park boasts 18 attractions including a 200ft (61-meter) erupting volcano and a vast selection of rides, slides, and all things watery.

Islands of Adventure is set around a small lake, so you can only approach the various islands from one direction or the other. Your actual route will probably depend on whether you have younger children, Harry Potter diehards or thrill-seeking teenagers in your party. Although the main focus of this park is on thrilling rides to suit all levels of courage, it also has shows and some wonderfully creative theme sets to explore. This route proceeds clockwise around the park, taking in the highlights.

MARVEL SUPER HERO ISLAND

Stroll through the Port of Entry, lined with shops and snack bars. When you reach the waterfront, turn left over the bridge and look up – you are now right underneath the first of the park's extreme thrill rides, the **Incredible Hulk Coaster ❶**. This high-speed roller coaster, recently revamped for yet bigger thrills, catapults you to high speeds in mere seconds. You'll zoom through a tunnel then be propelled out high over Marvel Super Hero Island, all to the tunes of a new score by Fall Out Boy's Patrick Stump.

Marvel Super Hero Island   *Coming face to face with King Kong*

After that, you may think you've lost your senses when you see the likes of Batman and Wonder Woman meandering through the streets, but the superheroes make several appearances throughout the day. There's more spinning and shaking in store at **Storm Force Accelatron ②** next door, while **Doctor Doom's Fearfall ③** rockets you 150 feet (45 meters) in the air and then drops you in stomach-churning intervals to the ground.

The Amazing Adventures of Spider-Man ④ is one of the park's most fantastic rides. This high-tech, 4-D experience is a great option for those who want the thrills but don't like roller coasters, although if you suffer from vertigo you might want to think twice.

Outstanding computer animation – seen through your night-vision goggles (3-D glasses) – combines with impressive motion simulation as you follow Spi-

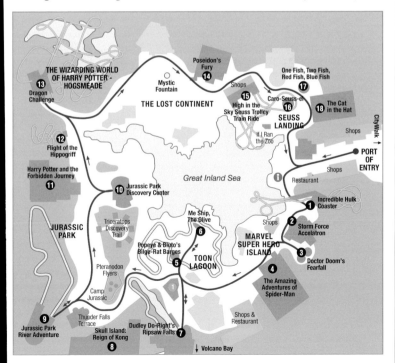

Meeting Spider–Man on the rooftops

der-Man's eerie rooftop journey through the deserted city in search of villains. When you take a 40-story plunge from the top of a skyscraper, it all seems terrifyingly real.

TOON LAGOON

As you enter the next island, you feel like you've walked right into the pages of the Sunday funnies. All the classic cartoon characters are here, from Betty Boop to Blondie and Dagwood to Beetle Bailey. If hunger strikes, step into the quick-serve **Blondie's**, see ①, and order a Dagwood – a fresh overstuffed sandwich reminiscent of those the character's husband eats in the comic strip.

Ride **Popeye & Bluto's Bilge-Rat Barges** ⑤ through churning white-water rapids – expect to get soaked. You'll also be fired on by water cannons from **Me Ship, The Olive** ⑥, a fun place for young children. More watery thrills are in store at **Dudley Do-Right's Ripsaw Falls** ⑦, a flume ride that plunges you down a steep, 75ft (23-meter) drop at high speed into the pond below – drenching guaranteed.

SKULL ISLAND: REIGN OF KONG

Next on your journey is **Skull Island: Reign of Kong** ⑧, a land designed around a single heart-thumper of a ride. The trackless 3-D newcomer, which brings a three-story-tall King Kong to life (you'll feel his breath), involves curved overhead screens, flying dinosaurs and, let's face it, lots of screaming.

JURASSIC PARK

Then on to the **Jurassic Park River Adventure** ⑨. After escaping from the claws of giant raptors and the jaws of T-Rex, your boat plunges through the dark to emerge with a big splash in the river below.

This island also contains a children's ride and playground, and the **Jurassic Park Discovery Center** ⑩, a hands-on interactive attraction where you can scan dinosaur fossils and create a dinosaur with your DNA.

CityWalk

Before, after, or instead of visiting the Universal Studios and Island of Adventure theme parks, consider spending time at CityWalk, a dining/shopping/entertainment plaza that connects the two. Entry is free except for admission to certain clubs. Lining the waterfront, CityWalk is packed with enough themed bars, restaurants, and nightclubs to keep you entertained every night of the week. They include Jimmy Buffett's Margaritaville, the world's largest Hard Rock Café, Pat O'Brien's Orlando (based on the New Orleans original), Bob Marley – A Tribute to Freedom, Red Coconut Club, and the multi-level club The Groove. CityWalk is generally open from 11am until 2am, and parking is free for Florida residents after 6pm.

Toothy raptor at Jurassic Park

It's all smiles on Flight of the Hippogriff

THE WIZARDING WORLD OF HARRY POTTER – HOGSMEADE

Grab a magic wand – or rather buy one at Ollivanders (the wand actually chooses you) – and join Harry, Hermione, and the rest of the gang in this realistic replica of Hogsmeade, decked out with snow-capped buildings and carts selling butterbeer. Try the regular and frozen, then debate which is best. The shopping is spirited, but most visitors flock here to ride **Harry Potter and the Forbidden Journey** ⓫. After winding through the Hogwarts School of Witchcraft and Wizardry while in line, you'll board a motion-based ride that seems to move in several directions while flying over the castle grounds. For a smaller buzz, choose **Flight of the Hippogriff** ⓬, a light roller coaster tied into the theme. For old-fashioned roller-coaster fun, try one or both of the **Dragon Challenge** ⓭ tracks, which intertwine. Both Chinese Fireball and Hungarian Horntail loop and twist like serpents' tails, turning you upside down several times in a variety of ways.

THE LOST CONTINENT

This quiet land is known more for Mythos, see page 114, one of the park's best restaurants, than entertainment. Still, **Poseidon's Fury** ⓮ draws on special effects in an ancient temple, including a walk through an inversion tunnel surrounded by swirling water.

SEUSS LANDING

The zany world of Dr. Seuss comes to life in this wonderful robustly hued island, one of the most creative sets in any theme park anywhere. The design is so true to the illustrations of the famous children's books that you won't find a single straight line – even the trees are crooked. Although the rides are mostly geared for kids, nostalgic adults love Seuss Landing just as much. Take your time strolling through here and enjoy all its delightful detail.

Get an overview from the **High in the Sky Seuss Trolley Train Ride** ⓯. Instead of traditional horses, you'll ride Dog-alopes, Cowfish, and Aqua Mop Tops on the **Caro-Seuss-el** ⓰. Steer a fish through squirting musical fountains in **One Fish, Two Fish, Red Fish, Blue Fish** ⓱. The highlight of Seuss Landing is undoubtedly **The Cat in the Hat** ⓲, where you ride through the topsy-turvy household of Dr Seuss' most famous character.

The Dolphin Days show at the Dolphin Theater

SEAWORLD AND DISCOVERY COVE

With a collection of fascinating marine animals – from penguins to sharks, manatees, and dolphins – SeaWorld and its sister park, Discovery Cove, offer a wholly different experience to Orlando's main theme parks.

> **PARK SIZE:** SeaWorld: 200 acres (81 hectares); Discovery Cove: 22 acres (9 hectares)
> **TIME:** One day for each park
> **START:** SeaWorld
> **END:** Discovery Cove
> **POINTS TO NOTE:** When you arrive at SeaWorld, take a few minutes to study the schedule of show times.

SeaWorld, which opened in 1973, is a laid-back, education-oriented marine park. Several thrill rides have been added in recent years, attracting an entirely new group of visitors. Still, the focus of the park is on the animals and the main sights are its animal shows and exhibits.

SeaWorld has been entangled in controversy in recent years following the release of *Black Fish*, a documentary which strongly criticized SeaWorld's treatment of marine mammals – in particular orcas – and questioned the very ethics of keeping them in captivity. SeaWorld's attendance figures and profits dropped drastically, and in 2016 SeaWorld announced that they would be ending their orca-breeding program, and that 'theatrical' killer-whale shows would be gradually phased out (Orlando's will cease in 2019).

SeaWorld has a more relaxed atmosphere than many theme parks. It invites meandering from one animal habitat to another in between shows, and lingering at your favorites. If you want to get as much as possible in during your visit, buy a Quick Queue add-on; there's a single-ride version plus another that gets you to the front of the line for seven high-demand experiences.

The shows you choose to see and/or the thrill rides you choose to experience will determine your route through SeaWorld. This route describes the highlights, moving in a generally clockwise direction. You can save money on 1-day tickets to SeaWorld by buying them online at www.seaworld.com. Multi-day and multi-park passes are also available. Download the SeaWorld Discovery Guide app, which does everything from help you find your

Flying high on Manta

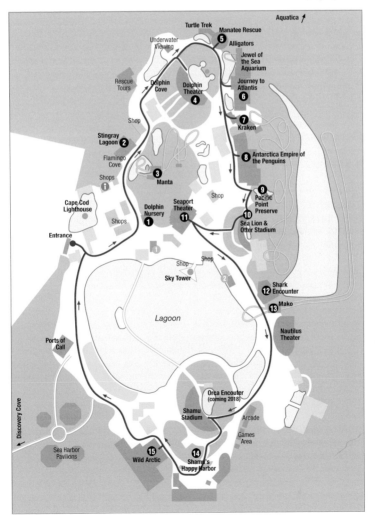

Aquatica

Turtle Trek
Manatee Rescue
5
Underwater
Viewing
Alligators
Jewel of
the Sea
Aquarium
Rescue
Tours
Dolphin
Cove
Dolphin
Theater
4
Journey to
Atlantis
6
Shop
7
Stingray
Lagoon **2**
Kraken
Flamingo
Cove
Antarctica Empire of
8 the Penguins
3
Shops
Manta
9
Pacific
Point
Preserve
Cape Cod
Lighthouse
Dolphin
Nursery
Seaport
Theater
Shop
10
Shops
1
11
Sea Lion &
Otter Stadium
Entrance
Shop
Shop
Sky Tower
2
Shark
12 Encounter
Lagoon
13 Mako
Nautilus
Theater
Ports of
Call
Discovery Cove
Orca Encounter
(coming 2018)
Shamu
Stadium
Arcade
Games
Area
Sea Harbor
Pavilions
15
Wild Arctic
14
Shamu's
Happy Harbor

Spotting turtles and tropical fish

car to displaying show times and wait times for rides.

SEAWORLD

Once inside the park entrance, pick up a map and study the show schedule. Try to stay late to watch *Electric Ocean*, an energetic, music-oriented sundown experience.

Sea of Shallows
As you leave the Port of Entry, you'll hit Sea of Shallows, home to three popular attractions as well as several 'Animal Connections' like the Dolphin Nursery and Flamingo Cove.

The **Dolphin Nursery ❶**, upgraded in 2017, shows mothers and babies together through large acrylic windows, and digital displays share information. Nearby at the **Stingray Lagoon ❷** you can put your hand into the shallow water to feel their smooth skin, but you'll have to be very quick as these fascinating creatures glide swiftly away.

Manta ❸ is located opposite. This popular roller coaster has riders move in the air as a manta ray does in water – including a face-first nosedive. Then stop in at the Manta Aquarium to see more than 200 rays.

Head on toward the **Dolphin Theater ❹**, where a new theatrical production called *Dolphin Days* replaced *Blue Horizons* in April 2017. The new show, still with acrobatic dolphin displays, has been reconfigured to convey a more environmentally friendly message (there's information about protecting animals in the wild, for instance). And while there's audience participation, tropical birds flying overhead, and acrobatic feats, *Dolphin Days* is more muted than its predecessor. Nearby, you can watch dolphins go about their business at the interactive **Dolphin Cove** and an underwater viewing area. For a few dollars you can buy some fish at feeding time and stroke the dolphins as you feed them.

Opposite the theater, you can examine two Florida natives, first at the alligator pond and behind it at **Manatee Rescue ❺**. This may be the closest you'll ever come to these elusive and endangered sea mammals. Go down into the underwater viewing area to get a look at their endearing faces.

Sea of Legends
Continue along to two big thrill rides. **Journey to Atlantis ❻** is a water coaster ride with a barrage of special effects, drops, and dips, ending in a 60ft (18-meter) soaking plunge that is super steep. Cobra rolls, vertical loops, and a G-force that keeps you glued to your seat at 65mph (100kph) are just a few reasons why **Kraken ❼** is named after mythology's scariest sea monster. This terrifying roller coaster also drenches you in its watery, eel-infested lair. As of summer 2017, Kraken was made yet more high-tech with the addition of virtual-reality technology.

A penguin-themed ride   _Mako, a ride of superlatives_

Sea of Ice

Antarctica: Empire of the Penguin

8 brings you into a world of icy caves. Choose the mild or thrill-packed version of this exciting ride with a glacially impressive design. Afterward, walk around to visit five species of penguin – including an underwater view – and watch more on the penguin cam. It's fun to watch these black-and-white creatures waddling over the ice, sliding down the snow mounds, diving, and swimming underwater at lightning speed.

Sea of Delight

A walk around **Pacific Point Preserve 9**, home to sea lions and seals, is amusing. They're not shy about demanding food with loud, persistent barking. You can also buy fish to feed them.

Facing the preserve is the **Sea Lion & Otter Stadium 10**, where the _Clyde & Seamore's Sea Lion High_ show is performed. The sea lions in the starring roles are perfect hams, but the otter and walrus action are welcome scene-stealers.

The nearby **Seaport Theater 11** – past Voyagers Smokehouse near Manta – is home to a land animal show, _Pets Ahoy_, featuring rescued cats, dogs, pigs, and other non-sea critters performing remarkable tricks.

Stretching along the waterfront, **The Seafire Grill**, see **1**, is a Tex-Mex stop. The **Spice Mill**, see **2**, has American food and dining on a deck overlooking the lake.

Sea of Mystery

Come to **Shark Encounter 12**, where these fearsome predators swim around and above you as you walk through a glass tunnel inside the aquarium. This 124ft (38-meter) tunnel is strong enough to support the weight of 372 elephants, a total of 2,232 tons. More than 200 species can be seen here and in the open pools outside. Other tanks hold lionfish, eels, barracudas, and more menacing creatures of the deep. You can watch them while you dine at the park's most upscale restaurant, Sharks Underwater Grill, see page 116.

While you're in the area, It's time for another thrill ride with **Mako 13**, a 'hypercoaster' billed as taller, longer, and faster than any other roller coaster in Orlando, with a 200ft (61-meter) drop, nearly a mile of track, and speeds of up to 73mph (118kmph). In other words, thrills don't get much bigger.

Up-close tours

Although they add to the bill, a guided tour will get you a closer look at the sea animals. SeaWorld's behind-the-scenes tour (from $29; 75 minutes; all ages) brings you backstage to learn how the trainers interact with rescued sea turtles and manatees, and also gets you up close with a penguin and a shark. Up-close tours (prices and lengths vary) offer interactive encounters with sharks, dolphins, penguins, sea lions, and walruses.

Swimming with dolphins at Discovery Cove

Sea of Fun

At Shamu Stadium, **Orca Encounter** – due to open in mid-2018 and billed as an 'educational' rather than a 'theatrical' show – will teach guests about orcas by witnessing them up close.

Behind the stadium, **Shamu's Happy Harbor ⓮** is a play area which also has a few kiddie rides. Like its real-world counterpart, **Wild Arctic ⓯**, home to a walrus and entertaining beluga whales, it feels quite remote from the rest of the park. You can also go on a polar expedition via a film and simulated helicopter ride. Continue back to the entrance.

DISCOVERY COVE

In a city where it often seems you battle the crowds from breakfast to bedtime, Discovery Cove (6000 Discovery Cove Way; tel: 407-513-4600; www.discoverycove.com; daily 9am–5pm) – an entirely separate park – offers a rare escape. Here admission is limited to 1300 guests a day, ensuring a relaxed, secluded environment. You must book well in advance (reservations are required) because the park is filled to capacity nearly every day.

At Discovery Cove you have the opportunity to swim with a dolphin. The experience includes learning hand signals, feeding the dolphins and swimming with them.

Discovery Cove offers many other attractions. There's a fantastic coral reef where you can snorkel among thousands of tropical fish and large stingrays, and a ray lagoon where you can stroke baby rays. You can float along a warm, lazy river that passes beneath waterfalls, over submerged ruins, and into three aviaries filled with exotic birds of all shapes and sizes. Walk through it and some will even perch on your arm, thanks to the cups of food provided by staff members. You can also just snorkel in the freshwater pool or relax on the sandy beaches.

Aquatica

SeaWorld has a water-themed water park, Aquatica (www.aquaticabyseaworld.com), nearby. True to form, the first slide you come to is the Dolphin Plunge, which shoots you right through a pool of Commerson's dolphins.

Food and drink

❶ SEAFIRE GRILL

The Waterfront, SeaWorld; $
Flame-grilled burgers are the top attractions here, with sandwiches and stir-fry also on the menu.

❷ SPICE MILL

The Waterfront, SeaWorld; $
Robust items like a buffalo chicken sandwich plus a variety of burgers. The lakeside deck is a relaxing spot for lunch or just to enjoy a beer and a snack.

Glittering Orlando cityscape

DOWNTOWN ORLANDO

*Downtown Orlando is the heart and soul of the city's arts community.
A visit here makes a refreshing change from the theme parks and
Disney characters. With a vibrant restaurant and nightlife scene too,
this is the perfect Orlando playground for adults.*

DISTANCE: 2 miles (3km)
TIME: Four to five hours
START: Heritage Square
END: Thornton Park
POINTS TO NOTE: You may want to
time your visit to take in the Sunday
Farmers' Market at Lake Eola.

Theme parks are so dominant in Central Florida that a large number of visitors think Disney Springs – which is part of Walt Disney World Resort and was for many years named Downtown Disney – and downtown Orlando are one and the same. Make sure to specify to taxi drivers that you want downtown Orlando, the city, and you won't be disappointed.

This route takes in the most exciting part of the city's commercial center, which is about 15 miles (24km) north of both the international airport and theme parks off I-4. The section known as the Downtown Arts District encompasses various museums and galleries; in addition, the route visits Lake Eola Park and the trendy Thornton Park neighborhood.

You can reach downtown Orlando by Lynx bus (www.golynx.com), car, or SunRail (www.sunrail.com), the area's light commuter rail. Service spans from DeBary in the north to Sand Lake Road to the south, with extensions further south to Osceola County in the works. SunRail operates mostly during commuting hours, with additional service during special events. Once you're Downtown, take the free Lymmo buses (www.golynx.com) from place to place; they run in four loops around the city's heart.

ORANGE COUNTY REGIONAL HISTORY

The route begins at Heritage Square, a bright modern plaza in the heart of Downtown. Street parking is limited, but garages nearby are reasonably priced.

Bordering the north side of the square, you'll find the **Orange County Regional History Center ❶** (65 E Central Boulevard; tel: 407-836-8500; www.thehistorycenter.org; Mon–Sat 10am–5pm, Sun noon–5pm). Constructed in 1927, this Greek Revival building served

Sculpture outside the History Center

as the county courthouse until 1999. Now an affiliate of the Smithsonian Institution, the museum houses four floors of interesting exhibits on the history of Orange County.

Starting on the fourth floor, you'll find displays on Florida's native people, the Seminoles, and the rural pioneers known as 'Crackers'. Note their recipes for baked possum and squirrel soup. Another room devoted to the citrus industry has some great kitschy memorabilia. The third floor takes an entertaining look at the Tin Can Tourists of the 1920s, and a more sobering view of how the coming of Walt Disney World changed Orlando from an agrarian, citrus-based economy to the tourist mecca it is today.

Across the hall, Courtroom B has been restored to its original state. The first case

in the United States in which a conviction was obtained using DNA evidence was tried in this room. Mass murderer Ted Bundy was also tried in the annex, and his name is scratched into the surface of the defense table. On the second floor a glass case holds the original manuscript for Jack Kerouac's *The Dharma Bums*, written on a rented manual typewriter while he was living in his mother's back porch apartment in Orlando in 1958.

DOWNTOWN ARTS DISTRICT

From Heritage Square, walk south along Magnolia Avenue. The core of the Downtown Arts District (www.orlandoslice.com) lies along several blocks between here and Orange Avenue. Many of the old storefronts have been brightly painted

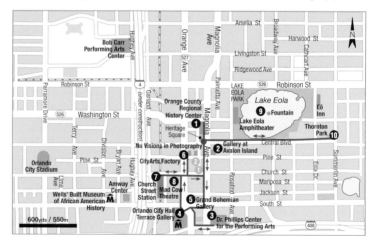

The Dr. Phillips Center   *Bold exhibit at the Grand Bohemian Gallery*

and renovated to house shops and galleries. The third Thursday of every month is a great time to visit, as Third Thursdays (www.3rdthu.com) are when about a dozen art galleries host an evening Gallery Walk from 6–9pm. Food and drink is often served, and new shows tend to open on this day.

At the corner with Pine Street, the Rogers building is the oldest commercial building in Orlando. It now houses the **Gallery at Avalon Island** ❷ (39 S Magnolia Avenue; tel: 407-803-6670; www.avalongallery.org; Tue–Sat noon–6pm) and other arts organizations. The gallery features local and international contemporary artists, with new shows opening every month.

Continue down Magnolia Avenue, stopping at **Le Gourmet Break**, see ❶, if you're in need of a snack, until you cross South Street to reach the state-of-the-art **Dr. Phillips Center for the Performing Arts** ❸ (445 S Magnolia Avenue; tel: 407-839-0119; www.drphillipscenter.org), a spectacular performance space and performing arts school. Exiting the venue, turn left on South Street, and walk to Orange Avenue and the **Orlando City Hall Terrace Gallery** ❹ (400 S Orange Avenue; tel: 407-246-4279; www.cityoforlando.net/arts; Thu–Sat 11am–6pm). It displays the work of Florida artists and hosts traveling exhibitions throughout the year.

Cross the street and walk north along Orange Avenue to reach the entrance to the **Grand Bohemian Gallery** ❺ (325 S Orange Avenue; tel: 407-581-4801; www.grandbohemiangallery.com; Mon 9.30am–5.30pm, Tue–Sat 9.30am–10pm, Sun 10am–3pm), located inside the Grand Bohemian Hotel. This small but superb gallery represents an eclectic range of artists, and is usually full of moneyed clients looking for their next investment.

More artworks are displayed in the hotel lobby and bar, with yet more on every floor. Take the elevator to the fifth floor, which is a small art museum in itself. In one corridor is a collection of paintings by Marcel Marceau called 'The Third Eye,' some featuring his character Bip. Not many people know the famous mime artist was also an accomplished painter.

Another corridor is lined with the original paintings by Larry Moore for the playbills for the Orlando Opera. Moore is known for his vivid Florida landscapes.

Sporting venues

The Orlando City Stadium (www.orlandocitysc.com/stadium) opened in 2017 as the newest addition to downtown Orlando's sporting landscape. It is home to the Orlando City Soccer and Orlando Pride soccer teams, has a capacity of 25,500, and its pitch is sunken 8ft (2.5 meters) below ground level to enhance viewing. The Amway Center arena (www.amwaycenter.com), opened in 2010, is another popular venue hosting sports events and concerts.

Lake Eola's farmers' market

In the Center Gallery are paintings by Dean Cornwell (1892–1960). Called the 'dean of American illustrators,' his work appeared in popular magazines like the Saturday Evening Post and Harpers Bazaar. He also illustrated the works of such authors as Ernest Hemingway and W. Somerset Maugham. Call 407-581-4801 to schedule an art tour.

Back on Orange Avenue, walk north past City Plaza, newly developed with a cinema and some trendy if non-spectacular restaurants. You're better off detouring to **Artisan Table**, see ❷ (22 W. Pine St., www.artisanstableorlando. com). On the corner of Pine and Orange is the vibrant **CityArts Factory** ❻ (29 S Orange Avenue; tel: 407-648-7060; www. cityartsfactory.com; Tue–Sat 11am–6pm), set in the former Phillips Theatre built in the 1920s. With several galleries in one place and free admission, it serves as a hub for the Downtown Arts District, promoting bohemian as well as upscale artists. The building also has a class-room and studio space. Upstairs there is a large area for hosting performances and events, with an adjacent lounge.

CHURCH STREET

Backtrack on Orange Avenue and turn right on Church Street, which leads into **Church Street Station** ❼, a two-block historic district around the old train depot. Most of the buildings date from the 1880s to early 1900s, or have had period architectural features incorpo-

rated into their renovation. This was once the big nightlife place in Orlando, but it suffered a decline in the 1990s and a series of new owners have failed to trans-form it to its former glory.

Outdoor tables are set along the cobbled pavements beneath gleam-ing wrought-iron galleries. Several high-ceilinged buildings are now home to atmospheric high-concept restaurants such as Ceviche. Peek into the window of the Cheyenne Saloon & Opera House, which was once a country-western bar and now opens only for private parties. Many other restaurants and bars are located in the surrounding streets.

The section of Church Street just north of the historical bit, called Church Street Marketplace, is equally packed with res-taurants and bars. The **Mad Cow Thea-tre** ❽ puts on good productions here, The Rusty Spoon, see page 115, serves some of the city's best farm-to-table meals, and the area's clubs attract swarms of party animals on weekend nights.

LAKE EOLA AND THORNTON PARK

Return to Magnolia, taking it left, and then take a right on Central Boulevard. This runs along the south side of **Lake Eola** ❾, the site of many city festivals and fire-works displays. The 43-acre (17-hectare) park is a recreational haven for Downtown residents, with a playground, café, and 0.9-mile (1.4km) path around the lake for strolling and jogging. You can also cruise the water in swan-shaped paddleboats.

Lake Eola in the sunshine　　　　*Al-fresco dining in Thornton Park*

An amphitheater on the west side of the lake is used for concerts and special events, and a variety of shops encourage browsing along Central Boulevard. On Sundays, a farmers' market takes place by the lake's southeast corner at Central and Eola Drive. In February, the Downtown Food and Wine Festival brings out the culinary curious, and in November the Fall Fiesta in the Park displays a variety of for-sale arts and crafts.

Beyond is the old Orlando neighborhood of **Thornton Park** ⑩, where new residential lofts and renovated cottages have joined the Craftsman-style bungalows and other historic homes. The 1923 Eö Inn (www.eoinn.com) overlooks Lake Eola and is now a boutique hotel. A string of trendy restaurants, bars, and shops line the main crossroads of Central Boulevard and Summerlin Avenue, making this a chic spot in the city for drinking and dining.

The fascinating Wells' Built Museum of African American History

SIDE TRIP

If you have time, consider also visiting the **Wells' Built Museum of African American History** (511 W South Street; tel: 407-245-7535; www.wellsbuiltmuseumofafricanamericanhistoryandculture.org; Mon–Fri 9am–4pm, Sat 10am–2pm). On the west side of I-4, this obscure museum contains memorabilia, photographs, and exhibits on the black musicians and artists who entertained in Downtown Orlando during the days of segregation. This 1920s hotel housed such notable performers as Ella Fitzgerald and baseball legend Jackie Robinson, and is one of the few lodging stops on the famed Chitlin Circuit still in existence.

Food and drink

① LE GOURMET BREAK
150 S Magnolia Avenue; tel: 407-371-9476; www.le-gourmet-break.com; $
Simple counter-service café serving authentic French specialties like crepes and quiches.

② ARTISAN TABLE
22 W Church Street; tel: 407-730-7499; www.artisanstableorlando.com; $$
Contemporary American fare with global influences served all day in a modern dining room.

Gold-framed paintings at the Orlando Museum of Art

LOCH HAVEN PARK

Downtown Orlando's cultural corridor continues 3 miles (5km) north in Loch Haven Park, an enclave of outstanding museums and performing arts venues separated from the surrounding streets by verdant grounds. Nearby are the lush landscapes of the Harry P. Leu Gardens.

DISTANCE: 2 miles (3km)
TIME: Half a day
START: Orlando Museum of Art
END: Harry P. Leu Gardens
POINTS TO NOTE: Apart from the Subway at the Science Center, there are no restaurants in or near Loch Haven Park, so make sure you bring some snacks if you plan to spend a long time in the museums or at Leu Gardens.

ORLANDO MUSEUM OF ART

Housed in a handsome circular-looking building (it's not really), the **Orlando Museum of Art ❶** (2416 N Mills Avenue; tel: 407-896-4231; www.OMArt.org; Tue–Fri 10am–4pm, Sat–Sun noon–4pm) stages 10 to 12 traveling exhibitions a year in addition to those from its permanent collection of contemporary, American, African, and ancient pre-Columbian art.

A towering glass sculpture by Dale Chihuly stands in the atrium at the entrance to the galleries. To the left is the Lakeview Promenade Gallery, lined with intriguing portraits in a variety of mediums, and a gallery of African Art with themed exhibitions ranging from textiles to vessels. This leads into the Art of the Ancient Americas gallery, with a fascinating collection of ceramic vessels and figures, gold jewelry, copper figurines, masks, and tiny carved beads as well as decorative and ritual objects from Central and South America dating back to 2000 BC.

The galleries to the right of the atrium contain a rotating collection of American art from the 18th century to the present, including landscapes, portraits, and traditional and contemporary sculpture. The museum's permanent collection includes works by Georgia O'Keeffe, John James Audubon, John Singer Sargent, and several American Impressionist painters.

ORLANDO THEATERS

Next to the art museum is the **Orlando Repertory Theatre ❷** (1001 E Princeton Street; tel: 407-896-7365; www.orlandorep.com), a familyoriented pro-

The state-of-the-art Orlando Science Center

fessional theater company whose productions are based on classic and contemporary children's literature. Across the parking lot you'll find a domed building housing the **Orlando Shakespeare Theater ❸** (812 E Rollins Street; tel: 407-447-1700; www.orlando shakes.org), which stages the Bard's classics as well as contemporary plays in its large and small theaters. It is also one of the main venues for the Orlando Fringe Festival (see page 71).

ORLANDO SCIENCE CENTER

A path beside the theater leads to the **Orlando Science Center ❹** (777 E Princeton Street; tel: 407-514-2000,

www.osc.org; school year Sun–Tue, Thu–Sun 10am–5pm, plus the first Wednesday of the month, summer daily 10am–5pm, extended hours Fri–Sat, observatory open seasonally). It contains dozens of hands-on exhibits spread over four levels plus a giant CineDome movie theater, a digital 3-D theater, and an observatory.

The exhibits appeal mainly to children (of varying ages). Among the highlights are KidsTown, an 11,000-sq-ft (1022-sq-meter) early childhood exhibit for children aged seven and under. Its seven zones are packed with interactive activities like water tables, a climbing structure, and a mini-play orange grove. Elsewhere, hands-on science displays

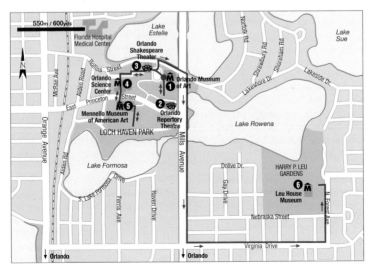

Mennello Museum of American Art gardens

involving dinosaur fossils, earthquakes, aerodynamics, and engineering fascinate in halls like DinoDigs, Our Planet, and the Kinetic Zone. The NatureWorks exhibit has a pond with turtles and alligators. The Crosby Observatory features a 10-inch (25.5cm) refractor telescope for sky-watching.

THE MENNELLO MUSEUM OF AMERICAN ART

For a safe way across the busy road, take the pedestrian bridge from the Science Center to the parking garage. From here it's a short walk to **The Mennello Museum of American Art ❺** (900 E Princeton Street; tel: 407-246-4278; www.mennellomuseum.org; Tue–Sat 10.30am–4.30pm, Sun noon–4.30).

This small but important museum features the permanent collection of Earl Cunningham, a self-taught artist who has been called one of the most innovative landscape painters of his gener-

ation. His bright palette and energetic scenes of forests and coastlines are full of life and well-observed detail, while his tiny, exquisitely rendered birds and people are reminiscent of L.S. Lowry.

Rotating additional exhibits feature other American artists. In the outdoor sculpture garden by the lake, large-scale sculptures are displayed for a year at a time via a series called Grounds for Exhibitions. Nearby, be sure to see the amazing southern live oak, called 'The Mayor', opposite the entrance by the parking area. More than a couple of centuries old, its enormous branches are so heavy they touch the ground.

LEU GARDENS

To visit some of Central Florida's finest gardens, you'll have to return to your car. The route is well signposted. Depending on where you've parked, drive east on E. Princeton Street to the end of Loch Haven Park and turn right on N. Mills Avenue. (If you're parked behind the Orlando Art Museum, exit by the museum and turn right directly onto N. Mills.) Then turn left at Virginia Drive and after about half a mile (800 meters), make a slight left at N. Forest Avenue, then turn left to stay on N. Forest.

The entrance to the **Harry P. Leu Gardens ❻** (1920 N Forest Avenue; tel: 407-246-2620; www.leugardens.org; daily 9am–5pm) is just beyond. Encompassing nearly 50 acres (20 hectares) on the shores of Lake Rowena, it con-

Where to park

The Orlando Museum of Art has a large parking lot behind the building, which also serves the theaters. You can walk to the Science Center from there. Alternatively, there are a limited number of parking spaces in front of The Mennello Museum of American Art, and a large parking garage opposite the Science Center, which is a short walk away.

Inside the Mennello Museum   *Strolling through colorful Leu Gardens*

tains a stunning array of features including native wetland, tropical stream, and desert gardens, as well as herb, vegetable, and citrus gardens, and the largest formal rose garden in Florida.

Leu Gardens is most famous for its camellias. With more than 2,000 specimens, it is the largest documented collection in eastern North America. Spread out beneath mature oaks in the North and South Woods, they bloom from October through March. From the boardwalk overlooking the lake, you can see alligators, heron, and a variety of shorebirds.

In the center of the grounds is the **Leu House Museum** (museum tours 10am–3.30pm, closed in July). Dating from 1888, and filled with fine period furniture and household items, it offers an intriguing look at the Central Florida lifestyle through the four families who owned it. Family treasures among the interesting artifacts in the Leu House Museum are a mourning wreath made of human hair, a top hat made of beaver fur, a spool bed, an Oliver typewriter (predecessor to the Olivetti), and a morning glory gramophone that still plays. The property was purchased in 1936 by Harry P. Leu, a rich businessman, and he and his wife developed the gardens, donating it to the city in 1961.

Orlando Fringe Festival

The two-week Orlando Fringe Festival (www.orlandofringe.org) takes over Loch Haven Park in late May every year and is the longest running of all the fringe festivals in the US. It aims to provide an accessible, affordable outlet for theater, music, dance, art, and madness of all types. Performances take place in the local theaters, and nightly outdoor concerts.

Performers come in all shapes and sizes from all over the world, and you will never know quite what to expect. You may get amateurs struggling with first-time nerves, or you may see the next big thing. It is all part of the fun. Imagine the Edinburgh Fringe only smaller and with guaranteed sunshine.

Tickets are available per show, and via passes that provide entry to several shows.

The Kids Fringe puts on around 45 child-friendly options.

Food and drink

Loch Haven Park lacks any restaurants or cafés, but the nearby Mills 50 District is loaded with pocket-friendly eateries including Black Rooster Taqueria, Hawkers, and Pig Floyd's, a short drive away. The only on-site option for refreshment is the Subway sandwich shop at the Science Center. A few blocks past Harry P. Leu Gardens, East End Market food hall has several food purveyors and communal seating, plus the table-service ramen shop Domu.

The iconic Orlando Eye

INTERNATIONAL DRIVE

Love it or hate it, I–Drive is one of Orlando's most important tourist thoroughfares. Along this wide boulevard you'll find theme parks, water parks, attractions, dinner shows, outlets, malls, and a host of shops and restaurants catering to every taste and budget.

DISTANCE: 9 miles (14km)
TIME: Thirty minutes to drive plus sightseeing and shopping time
START: Vineland Avenue
END: Oakridge Road
POINTS TO NOTE: The area around the Convention Center can become hopelessly jammed when a big show is in town.

International Drive is for sure the area's most tourist-oriented stretch of road. This isn't surprising, as it serves the visitor vortex of the Orange County Convention Center. You'll find I-Drive, as it's commonly called, alternately smart or somewhat tacky, depending on the hotels, shops, and attractions along any given stretch.

Although I-Drive's southern boundary is Highway 192, there is nothing much of interest except more hotels and open spaces waiting to be developed until you reach Vineland Avenue, where our route begins. It is anchored at either end by two of the city's outlet malls, one

big, one small, so plan to bag some bargains on this route.

If you're coming from I-4, take exit 68 east to reach **Orlando Vineland Premium Outlets ❶** (8200 Vineland Avenue; tel: 407-238-7787; www.premiumout lets.com/outlet/orlando-vineland; Mon–Sat 10am–11pm, Sun until 9pm). Set around an interior open-air court, it features such designer names as Armani, Ralph Lauren, Salvatore Ferragamo, and Calvin Klein among its 110 stores, plus an Elie Tahari outlet and an outparcel with, among others, Tommy Bahama.

From the mall, drive north on I-Drive. Central Florida Parkway divides SeaWorld from its sister park, Discovery Cove (see page 58). Also nearby is SeaWorld's **Aquatica ❷** (5800 Water Play Way; tel: 407-545-5550; www.aquaticabysea world.com; hours vary by season). Aquatica's signature attraction is the Dolphin Plunge, which sends visitors in clear tubes through an underwater world full of black-and-white Commerson's dolphins. The park has some killer water slides, along with a relaxing beach, a huge surf pool, a lazy river, and colorful kiddie play

Advertisements flank International Drive

areas. Its newest thrill is Ihu's Breakaway Falls with a 40ft (12-meter) vertical fall.

BEACHLINE EXPRESSWAY TO SAND LAKE ROAD

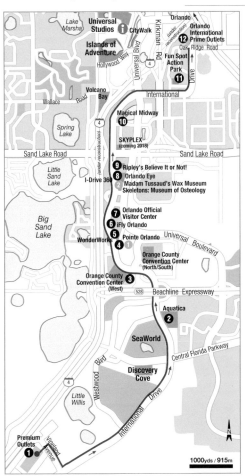

Cross under 528, the airport toll road also known as the Beachline Expressway. The nicest stretch of I-Drive runs between here and Sand Lake Road, along a wide landscaped boulevard. A whole lot of construction has brought yet more attractions and restaurants to this stretch of I-Drive, and more is underway.

The road curves west between the massive south and west concourses of the **Orange County Convention Center** ❸ (9899 and 9800 International Drive; tel: 800-345-9845; www.occc.net). With more than 7 million sq ft (650,000 sq meters), including 2.053 million sq ft (190.7 sq meters) of exhibition space, it consistently ranks as among the largest in the country. Expect heavy traffic during big conventions.

On the right, wedged between I-Drive and Universal Boulevard, is **Pointe Orlando** ❹ (9101

Treading carefully at WonderWorks

International Blvd; tel: 407-248-2838; www.pointeorlando.com; Oct–May Mon–Sat noon–10pm, Sun noon–8pm, June–Sept Sun–Thu noon–8pm, Fri–Sat noon–9pm), a smart multilevel shopping and dining center with several high-end chain restaurants like Capital Grille and Tommy Bahama's Tropical Café and Emporium. **Taverna Opa**, see ❶, is loud but has fabulous Greek food and infectiously fun live entertainment. Valet parking is free in the evenings for some restaurants. If you have teens in tow, don't miss Main Event, a modern arcade with bowling, pool, and a virtual-reality game.

The upside-down building alongside is **WonderWorks** ❺ (9067 International Drive; tel: 407-351-8800; www.wonder worksonline.com; daily 9am–midnight), a wacky world of optical illusions, tricks, and interactive exhibits spread over four floors. It's not as shiny (nor as expensive) as the theme parks, but it's good fun for adults as well as kids, with an inversion tunnel, bed of nails, and many other amusing exhibits.

Getting around

Even if you don't have a car, I-Drive is easy to traverse, as the reasonably priced I-Ride Trolley (www.iridetrolley.com) runs north and south from 8am to 10.30pm, with stops at more than 100 locations. Single fares are $2, kids aged 3–9 $1. There are also unlimited ride passes ranging from one day ($5) to 14 days ($18).

iFly Orlando ❻ (6869 International Drive; tel: 407-903-1150; www.iflyworld. com/orlando) is an indoor skydiving experience where you float on a column of air in a vertical wind tunnel.

Set back off the road beside Austrian Row is the **Orlando Official Visitor Center** ❼ (8723 International Drive; tel: 407-363-5872; www.visitorlando.com; daily 8.30am–6.00pm). Be aware that the center is moving to a new site at 8102 I-Drive at the end of 2017. You can pick up free maps, visitor guides, brochures, and discount coupons to restaurants and attractions; buy tickets for the theme parks and the I-Ride Trolley; and get directions. Helpful staff are on hand.

Keep heading north toward the giant Ferris wheel – the official Coca-Cola **Orlando Eye** (www.officialorlandoeye. com), a high-tech slow-moving ride with expansive views. It's at the heart of **I-Drive 360** ❽ (8375 International Drive; www.i-drive360.com), a growing complex with assorted tourist attractions, restaurants, and bars. Here you'll find a **Madame Tussaud's** wax museum (www.madametussauds.com); the modern **SeaLife Aquarium** (www.visitsea life.com/orlando), with clever underwater areas designed for selfies; and **Skeletons: Museum of Osteology** (www. skeletonmuseum.com), with the bones of more than 400 real animals. Bring kids to the Sugar Factory (www.sugar factory.com) for oversized desserts. If you're all adult, opt for the Spanish fare at **Tapa Toro**, see ❷.

Ripley's Believe It or Not!   *Family fun at Fun Spot Action Park*

Further north on the right, a tilting building holds the Orlando branch of the famed **Ripley's Believe It or Not!** 🅖 (8201 International Drive; tel: 407-363 4418; www.ripleysorlando.com; daily 9am–midnight). This aptly named 'Odditorium' is filled with bizarre exhibits collected by writer and cartoonist Robert Ripley, who traveled the world in the 1920s–40s. A lot of the displays seem dated today – animal and human deformities, tribal adornments and the like no longer seem shocking in our world of high-tech special effects. Still, there are some curiosities to be found among the more dubious displays.

NORTH OF SAND LAKE ROAD

The next stretch of I-Drive is characterized by a string of budget hotels, restaurants, and discount outlets. The mile after that offers many options for thrill-seekers. **Magical Midway** 🅞 (14 7001 International Drive; tel: 407-370-5353; www.magicalmidway.com) has elevated go-kart tracks, classic midway rides, and the Slingshot bungee and Star Flyer tower rides.

Turn left on Universal Boulevard for Universal Studios (see page 50), Islands of Adventure (see page 54), CityWalk (see page 56), and the Universal Complex's new water park, Volcano Bay (see page 54), a lush island-themed water park. Young families might want to take a later left up Grand National Drive to reach **Fun Spot Action Park** 🅛 (5700 Fun Spot Way; tel: 407-363-3867; www.fun-spot.com; daily 10am or 2pm–midnight), with

a sister location in Kissimmee (see page 78). Here you'll have old-fashioned fun with bumper cars and boats, go-karts, and all kinds of thrill rides.

Alternatively, carry on along I-Drive into a world of shopping. The biggie here is **Orlando International Prime Outlets** 🅛 (4951 International Drive; tel: 407-352-9600; www.premiumoutlets.com/outlet/orlando-international), a sprawling open-air mall anchored by Last Call and Off 5th, with about 200 outlet and factory stores including Vince, Ted Baker, and St. John.

Food and drink

🅐 TAVERNA OPA
Pointe Orlando; tel: 407-351-8660; www.opaorlando.com; $$
Mash your hummus at the table before indulging in a fine Greek feast, and prepare to have a great time, too. Between courses, guests watch – or join – a lively belly dancer, and many participate in a Zorba dance around the dining room, tossing up white napkins and yelling *Opa*! It sounds cheesy, but it's actually incredibly fun.

🅑 TAPA TORO
I-Drive 360, 8441 International Drive, Ondo; tel: 407-226-2929; www.tapatoro.restaurant; $$
Sit by the paella pit and watch the chefs make this Spanish restaurant's signature dish, or choose an indoor or outdoor table for tapas and Spanish and American entrées.

KISSIMMEE AND CELEBRATION

With its low-cost hotels and proximity to Disney World, Kissimmee is the base for many visitors. The minor attractions here provide some entertainment between visits to the big theme parks, but if you want more still, make the journey to LEGOLAND.

DISTANCE: 57 miles (92km)
TIME: One to two days
START: Celebration
END: LEGOLAND
POINTS TO NOTE: Because of its closeness to Walt Disney World, US 192 is almost always busy, especially the nearer you get to I-4, so allow extra time to reach your destination.

South of the city limits and adjacent to Disney World, Kissimmee blends seamlessly into Orlando. It sprawls along US 192, also known as the Irlo Bronson Memorial Highway, one of the area's main tourist drags. Lined with more chain hotels, restaurants, and gaudy souvenir shops than you can count, this busy road also serves the clusters of vacation homes, many quite tasteful, and most of which are a short drive from the main sights. Watch for the brightly colored guide markers along West US 192, which will help you locate hotels and attractions. If you're staying in the central or eastern part of Kissimmee,

the Osceola Parkway (Toll Road 522) leads directly into Walt Disney World Resort. It's worth the toll to avoid the traffic on US 192 and I-4.

Kissimmee grew up as a center for the region's ranchers and farmers, offering a bit of fun for the family when they came to town for the cattle market or rodeo. Although those days are rapidly disappearing, you'll still see cattle grazing alongside new holiday-home developments just a couple of miles south of town. This tour travels east from I-4, where Kissimmee's historic downtown, rodeo grounds, and Lake Toho are a reminder of the region's rural roots.

CELEBRATION

First, however, make a detour to the town of **Celebration** ❶, a place where small-town idealism meets new urbanism. Walt Disney was fascinated with the idea of building a town that would foster community life and environmental principals using the latest technological advances. He thought about every aspect of town planning, from schools

Neat streets in Disney–designed Celebration

to waste disposal to layouts that would encourage neighborly interaction.

Celebration was based on Disney's model for a town, but construction didn't start until the late 1990s, nearly 30 years after his death. Though it was laid out on land owned by the company, contrary to popular belief, it was not built for Disney employees. The first residents were chosen by lottery. In the early phases, each house was different, based on vernacular styles from across the country. The result is a bright, shiny, neat-as-a-pin town. The attention to detail and well-conceived planning makes a welcome relief from the brash anarchy of both US 192 and International Drive, where the only driving tenet behind construction seems to be bigger,

better, louder. Disney no longer owns Celebration, but the town, now grown up, is still worth a visit.

From Highway 192, turn south on Celebration Avenue (from I-4, take exit 62 and turn left onto Celebration Boulevard) and follow signs to Market Street. This is the heart of town, curving prettily around a small lake. It's a pleasant place to stroll, browse in the shops, or have a coffee or bite to eat in one of several good restaurants. The **Market Street Café** ① has a lake view.

Several top architects were hired to design the community buildings. At the top of Market Street is **Charles Moore's Preview Center**, the town's tallest building (Bank of America now occupies the ground floor). It recalls the

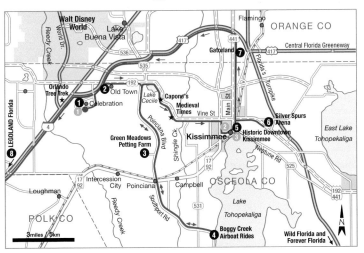

Enjoying a drink in Old Town

storm lookout towers used to mark new real estate developments in Florida's early 'wildcat' days.

Opposite is the red-brick **town hall** with its 52 white columns, designed by Philip Johnson. Next door, postmodernist architect Michael Graves designed the **post office** with outdoor mailboxes to facilitate contact among residents. Down by the lake, the twin spires of Cesar Pelli's cinema soar above the playful interactive fountain.

Celebration hosts frequent family-friendly events, many free, including snowfalls (think: bubbles!) with caroling in winter. For details, plus a list of restaurants, visit www.celebrationtown center.com.

Outdoor activities

In recent years, eco-tourism and facilities for athletic thrills have popped up around Kissimmee and its Osceola County environs. Among these are **Forever Florida** (www.foreverflorida.com), with nature tours and a fabulous variety of zip-line runs; **Orlando Tree Trek** (www.orlandotreetrek.com), with adult and children's rope courses; and **Wild Florida** (https://wildfloridairboats.com), with a gator and wildlife park. Sprawling resort complexes are home to golf courses with golf schools and high-tech learning facilities. Several vendors offer daybreak hot-air-balloon rides too. Visit www.experiencekissimmee.com for ideas.

OLD TOWN

Returning to reality on US 192 comes as quite a shock after even a short time in Celebration. Luckily Old Town (5770 W. Hwy 192; daily 10am–11pm) is just down the road. To put it in movie terms, it's like going from *The Truman Show* to *Happy Days*.

Not to be confused with downtown Kissimmee, Old Town is a family-friendly shopping, dining, and entertainment attraction with a 1950s vibe. Its brick-paved main street is lined with specialty shops and attractions, such as the Happy Times Arcade and the Mortem Manor haunted house. With '50s tunes setting the mood, adults enjoy strolling around, perhaps with a root beer for old times' sake.

Anchoring **Old Town** ❷ at one end are several thrill rides, including an iconic Ferris wheel which can be seen for several miles. (You'll eye the V-shaped towers of the Sling Shot, too, but that's not officially Old Town's.) At the other end are traditional fairground rides, games, and entertainment. Children especially enjoy The Great Magic Hall and the Rootin & Jootin's Shootin' Alley. More thrills are right next door at Fun Spot, with a race track, bumper cars, a scary bungee-jump attraction, and a new wooden roller coaster.

The highlight is the Saturday Nite Classic Car Cruise, when a parade of classic cars motors through Old Town (there's a Friday Nite Cruise too, for 'muscle' cars).

Airboat rides are an essential Florida experience

People line up along Main Street to watch the cruise, which begins at 8.30pm. Live entertainment plays until 11pm.

On cruise days the automobiles are lined up on display along Trophy Row from early afternoon on. Even if you're not that keen on cars, the shiny paintwork, chrome, and interiors of classic models in immaculate condition is impressive to see.

SMALL-TIME PLEASURES

Just off US 192 is Lake Tohopekaliga. Since few can pronounce its Indian name, which means 'sleeping cat', it's better known as Lake Toho. Lake Toho is part of the Kissimmee chain of lakes, which forms the headwaters to the Florida Everglades. There's no better way to explore it than from the water on a traditional Florida means of transport, an airboat.

Turn right on Poinciana Boulevard, which runs south out of the city. If you have small children you may want to make a detour on the way to **Green Meadows Petting Farm ❸** (1368 S Poinciana Boulevard; tel: 407-846-0770; www.greenmeadowsfarm.com; daily 9.30am–4pm, last tour starts 2.30pm), where they can milk a cow, have a pony ride, and enjoy other activities on a two-hour tour.

For the airboat rides, it's a 19-mile (30-km) drive from US 192 to the southwest shore of the lake. Poinciana Boulevard eventually becomes Southport

Road, which leads to Southport Park, the peaceful location of **Boggy Creek Airboat Rides ❹** (2001 E Southport Road; tel: 877-304-3239; www.bcairboats.com; daily 9am–5.30pm). No reservations are needed for the 30-minute rides, which run continuously throughout the day. Southport Park also has a Native American village experience; Romp-in-the-Swamp, where guests can drive an airboat; glamping; and a fossil dig.

Airboats are a thrilling way to experience the natural environment of the Central Florida Everglades. Piloted by master captains, they glide over the shallow surface of the lake, reaching speeds of more than 50 mph (80 kph), or putter beside grassy hammocks and into narrow, swampy glades between the cypress trees in search of wildlife.

Alligators are the prime animal everyone comes to see, but these wetlands also harbor turtles, snakes, bald eagles, osprey, rare snail kites, pelicans, sandhill cranes, and a host of migrating birds. On night tours you hunt for alligators who in turn are hunting their prey.

HISTORIC DOWNTOWN KISSIMMEE

Return to US 192 the way you came and turn right to continue the route. Fans of roadside Americana are in for a treat before they reach the historic downtown area. This tourist-heavy stretch of Kissimmee has some of the best kitsch storefronts in the country. Look for the citrus market shaped like a giant orange,

Historic Downtown Kissimmee at night

aptly named Orange World (www.orange world192.com), and enormous mermaids, wizards, alligators and the like beckoning you in to souvenir shops, mini-golf, and attractions. The main road is lined with chain restaurants, although in-the-know foodies go into the residential communities to seek out authentic Puerto Rican meals.

Watch for brown signs directing you to Kissimmee's historic district. Turn right on John Young Boulevard, then left on Emmett Street, which brings you through a pretty old residential neighborhood before swinging left onto Broadway. This is the start of **Historic Downtown Kissimmee ❺**, which has been self-sprucing-up lately.

Here you'll find a few antiques shops and art galleries, as well as the fabulously redeveloped lakefront park, which is a true community center. It has floating brick docks, a spray park, and tributes to history, and is also the locale for a weekly farmers' market (Tuesdays 3–7pm), a monthly food-truck event, and Friday night outdoor family movies. The old storefronts have gotten more attractive in recent years, especially along Broadway and Dakin Avenue, where a spattering of trendy restaurants, cocktail lounges, and wine bars have taken up residence. Look for the mural on Makinson Hardware depicting the town's rural days. **Savion's Place**, see ❷, is a nice spot for a bite with its American and Caribbean flavors, or grab a hot dog from **Willy's Wieners**, see ❸.

SILVER SPURS RODEO

Continue north on Main Street back to US 192. If the rodeo is in town, turn right to reach Osceola Heritage Park, home of the Silver Spurs Arena. Twice a year in February and June, Kissimmee hosts the **Silver Spurs Rodeo ❻** (tel: 321-697-3495; www.silverspursrodeo.com), the largest rodeo east of the Mississippi.

Professional riders compete indoors in events such as bull riding, steer wrestling, and barrel racing over three days. There are rodeo clowns, rodeo queens and displays of horsemanship that celebrate the area's long cattle-ranching heritage.

GATORLAND

Take Main Street north of US 192 and it becomes the Orange Blossom Trail, leading to one of Orlando's oldest attractions. **Gatorland ❼** (14501 S Orange Blossom Trail; tel: 407-855-5496; www.gatorland. com; daily 10am–5pm) was started in 1949 by Kissimmee cattle rancher Owen Godwin. It's a theme park with a focus on education and conservation; Gatorland also works with the University of Florida on alligator research projects.

Classic attractions here include the Gator Jumparoo show, where the enormous reptiles leap out of the water to grab their dinner, and the Gator Wrestlin' Show. The adventurous can zip line over trees and alligators, while the education-oriented might sign up for the 'Trainee for a Day' experience. Gatorland

LEGOLAND Florida   *Animal-themed ride at LEGOLAND*

also has displays of deadly snakes and other wildlife including a 300-pound (136kg) Galapagos tortoise, panthers, and bobcats.

LEGOLAND FLORIDA

LEGOLAND's Florida complex lies about 40 miles south of Kissimmee in Winter Haven. Take the Highway 417 toll road (just north of Gatorland) to I-4, then take I-4 West to US 27 (exit 55). From there, FL-540, Cypress Gardens Boulevard in Winter Haven, will lead you to **LEGOLAND Florida** ❽ (One Legoland Way; tel: 877-350-5346; www.legoland.com; hours vary), a haven for children aged two to 12.

The entire theme park, including the adjacent water park and two related hotels, is designed to look as if it is made out of the namesake plastic building blocks. In addition, there are 28,000 real LEGO models on show – made from a staggering 58 million+ bricks. Allow a full day, plus maybe an overnight, if you're traveling with small children.

The park is divided into 11 themed sections, and more are added regularly. Highlights include Miniland USA, with amazing models from around the country; LEGO Technic, with a coaster and Wave Racer personal watercraft; DUPLO Valley, which is great for toddlers; and Cypress Gardens, a well-maintained collection of native plants and flowers paying tribute to LEGOLAND's predecessor.

Gator Wrestlin' Show

Shady Central Park

WINTER PARK

Although it lies just north of downtown Orlando, Winter Park seems a world away from the theme parks and commercial center. With its oak-lined brick streets, upscale shops and restaurants, and handsome old neighborhoods, it's a refreshing change of pace from the tourist-oriented city.

> **DISTANCE:** 2.5 miles (4km)
> **TIME:** Three hours plus museum/shopping time
> **START:** Morse Museum
> **END:** Cornell Fine Arts Museum
> **POINTS TO NOTE:** The museums close Mondays.

Surrounded by large lakes, Winter Park was founded in 1881 as a winter resort for northerners. The Amtrak station and railroad tracks running through the heart of town are reminders that these early, wealthy visitors came by train.

As the citrus-growing business thrived, so did the town, and Winter Park developed a lifestyle of gracious homes and fine cultural institutions that remains today. Rollins College, an elite, private institution named for one of the city founders, is a liberal arts institution on a beautiful, serene campus.

Each year in March, the city hosts the Winter Park Sidewalk Art Festival. The three-day event is one of the most prestigious outdoor arts festivals in the country. More than 225 artists from around the world and 350,000–400,000 visitors attend. For more information, visit www.wpsaf.org.

In a world of ever-increasing chains, Winter Park also stands out for its high-quality, one-off shops and restaurants. Park Avenue, the main thoroughfare, has around 140 stores and galleries, as well as cafés, wine bars, and fine dining. It's divided into a north and south part, with the center on Morse Avenue.

Street parking can be tough to find, but there is free all-day parking in lots of garages on Canton Avenue by the railroad tracks, and across the tracks on either side of Morse Boulevard at New York Avenue.

CHARLES HOSMER MORSE MUSEUM OF AMERICAN ART

The route begins at the **Charles Hosmer Morse Museum of American Art** ❶ (445 N Park Avenue; tel: 407-645-5311; www.morsemuseum.org; Tue–Sat 9.30am–4pm, Sun 1–4pm). From lamps to pottery, jewelry, paintings, and

Tiffany lamps on display at the Charles Hosmer Morse Museum

art glass, it contains the world's most comprehensive collection of works by Louis Comfort Tiffany (1848–1933). An expansive wing added in 2011 features exhibitions tied to Laurelton Hall, the late artist's Long Island, New York, home. Leaded glass windows, custom furnishings, and the architecture itself – plus the Fountain Court reception hall – are all on display.

A museum highlight is the Tiffany Chapel, designed by the artist himself for the World's Columbian Exposition in Chicago in 1893. The Byzantine-style interior with its carved arches and intricate glass mosaics covering every inch of the pillars, altar, and baptismal font is simply stunning, while an enormous cross-shaped electrified chandelier hangs overhead. Free tours are available using your own mobile phone.

PARK AVENUE

Stroll south along Park Avenue. The eclectic range of stores and galleries is an invitation to browsing and window-shopping. A few to watch for include the **Scott Laurent Collection** (www.scottlaurentcollection.com), a gallery of contemporary art and furnishings; **Synergy** (www.synergysportswear.com), with a large collection of lifestyle clothing and comfort shoes; and **Be on Park** (http://beonpark.com), with designer jewelry and local art.

Park Avenue is often said to be European in style, with its cobbled street lined with sidewalk tables. But many of its two-

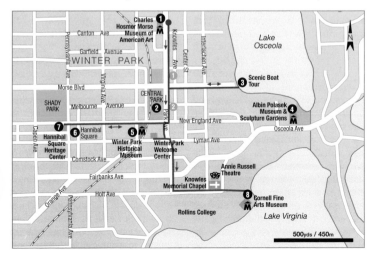

Stores and galleries line Park Avenue

story buildings look right out of 1920s America. A good place to fortify yourself with a coffee or ice cream is at the **Briarpatch Restaurant**, see ❶, where tables with bright umbrellas are set across the street from a park with beautiful oaks draped in Spanish moss. If you'd prefer a craft cocktail, a glass of Italian wine, or Orlando's best pasta, stop instead at the indoor-outdoor Prato, see page 118, for progressive Italian fare. **Bosphorus**, see ❷, which serves Turkish cuisine, is a must for its puffy *lavash* bread.

On the opposite side of the street, shady **Central Park** ❷ with its flower gardens and bandstand adds to the village-like atmosphere. There are often free concerts here on weekends. The park stretches for several blocks, with the railroad tracks running along the western side.

SCENIC BOAT TOUR

Turn east down Morse Boulevard and follow it to its end at Lake Osceola. Here, the **Scenic Boat Tour** ❸ (312 E Morse Blvd; tel: 407-644-4056; www.scenic boattours.com; daily 10am–4pm) shows you Winter Park from a different perspective, with guides giving an entertaining commentary along the way. The one-hour cruise sails along three of the area's chain of lakes and through the historic canals that link them; these were dug in the late 1800s for logging operations and today are solely used for pleasure boats.

After passing several gorgeous homes – many of these large mansions were mere summer retreats for wealthy families – you see the **Albin Polasek Museum & Sculpture Gardens** ❹ (633 Osceola Avenue; tel: 407-647-6294; www.polasek.org; Tue–Sat 10am–4pm, Sun 1–4pm). The Czech-American sculptor retired to this estate, and you can glimpse some of his works in the gardens. The museum contains many more of his paintings, drawings, and sculptures in addition to antiquities from his private collection.

The cruise then heads into the lush and overgrown Fern Canal which progresses into Lake Virginia. From here you can see some of the landmarks of Rollins College, looking very pretty and peaceful from the water.

HANNIBAL SQUARE

After the cruise, return to Park Avenue. Turn left and carry on to the end of Central Park, then turn right on New England Avenue. Across the tracks, opposite the park's southwest corner, is the site of the Saturday farmers' market. The small brick building alongside houses the **Winter Park History Museum** ❺ (200 W New England Avenue; tel: 407-647-8180; www.wphistory.org; Thu–Fri 11am–3pm, Sat 9am–1pm, Sun 1–4pm) with photographs, artifacts, and other exhibits on the community.

More boutique stores and restaurants line the next two blocks to **Han-**

Hannibal Square exhibit *Colorful clothing at Cornell Fine Arts Museum*

nibal Square ❻. This was the heart of the black community, who moved here in the 1880s to work in railroad and domestic-service jobs in the growing Winter Park community. A mural depicts a historic moment in 1887 when citizens crossed the railroad tracks to cast their votes and elected two African-American aldermen to Winter Park's town council.

In the next block, the **Hannibal Square Heritage Center** ❼ (642 W New England Avenue; tel: 407-539-2680; www.hannibalsquareheritagecenter.org; Tue–Thu noon–4pm, Fri noon–5pm, Sat 10am–2pm) has exhibits, photographs, and oral histories gathered from members of the community, and hosts traveling exhibitions.

ROLLINS COLLEGE

Return to Park Avenue and continue south. A detour right along Lyman Avenue leads you to the **Winter Park Welcome Center and Chamber of Commerce** (151 W Lyman Avenue; tel: 407-644-8281; www.cityofwinterpark.org), where you can pick up some maps and information.

Park Avenue ends at the grounds of Rollins College. Founded in 1885, it is Florida's oldest college. The attractive campus, with its original Spanish-Mediterranean-style buildings, spreads along the shores of Lake Virginia. Notice the Walk of Fame near the entrance, made of stepping stones gathered from places linked to famous historical figures.

Turn left on Holt Avenue and follow it to its end on the shores of the lake, where you can visit another of Winter Park's leading cultural attractions. **Cornell Fine Arts Museum** ❽ (1000 Holt Avenue; tel: 407-646-2526; www.rollins.edu/cfam; Tue 10am–7pm, Wed–Fri 10am–4pm, Sat noon–5pm, Sun 1–5pm) has an excellent collection of European and American paintings, sculpture, and decorative art from the Renaissance to contemporary times, with changing exhibitions and artists' talks.

Also on campus are the Annie Russell Theatre and the Knowles Memorial Chapel, connected by a loggia. Both buildings were built in 1931–2 and feature on the US National Register of Historic Places.

Food and drink

❶ **THE BRIARPATCH RESTAURANT**
252 N Park Avenue; tel: 407-628-8651; www.thebriarpatchrestaurant.com; $
A wholesome spot for coffee or ice cream, as well as full meals. Watch the passing scene from the sidewalk tables. Open daily for breakfast and lunch.

❷ **BOSPHORUS**
108 S Park Avenue; tel: 407-644-8609; http://bosphorousrestaurant.com; $$$
Serving Turkish cuisine, this popular restaurant is open for both lunch and dinner.

Bald eagle at the Audubon Center

NORTH OF ORLANDO

Just a few miles north of downtown Orlando, hotels and tourist attractions give way to the real world of central Florida. You'll find small, sleepy towns, natural springs, and state parks that harbor a wealth of wildlife, from fearsome alligators to gentle, lumbering manatees.

> **DISTANCE:** 30 miles (48km) from Eatonville to Blue Springs State Park direct
> **TIME:** One day
> **START:** Eatonville
> **END:** Blue Springs State Park
> **POINTS TO NOTE:** Stop off at Maitland on your way, or combine your trip with a visit to nearby Winter Park.

A good way to balance the surreal world of the theme parks is to visit the real world of the natural parks, where you can enjoy the great outdoors and see some of central Florida's natural springs and amazing wildlife. This route provides some suggestions that are right on Orlando's doorstep; most nearby nature parks are in Seminole County, which markets its sites as Orlando North.

EATONVILLE

Eatonville is the oldest African-American township in the country, founded in 1883. Although most of its original buildings are now gone, you can visit the humble **Zora Neale Hurston National Museum of Fine Arts** ❶ (227 E Kennedy Blvd; tel: 407-647-3307; www.zoranealehurstonmuseum.com; Mon–Fri 9am–4pm), dedicated to the town's most famous daughter. An author and folklorist, Hurston wrote about her early life in Eatonville in her novels *Their Eyes Were Watching God* and *Dust Tracks on a Road*.

AUDUBON CENTER FOR BIRDS OF PREY

Drive east along Kennedy Boulevard to East Street. Turn left on East Street, and after three blocks turn left on Audubon Way. This leads to the **Audubon Center for Birds of Prey** ❷ (1101 Audubon Way; tel: 407-644-0190; fl.audubon.org/audubon-center-birds-prey; Tue–Sun 10am–4pm). A nonprofit raptor rehabilitation center, it rescues and cares for more than 600 injured, sick, and orphaned birds of prey each year.

Maitland Art Center   *Bright designs at the Telephone Museum*

MAITLAND

Return to East Street, turn left, and follow the road around the shores of Lake Sybelia. Turn right on Packwood Avenue. Midway down this short street is the **Maitland Art Center** ❸ (231 W Packwood Avenue; tel: 407-539-2181; www.maitlandartcenter.org; Tue–Sun 11am–4pm).

The center was founded as an art colony in the 1930s–1950s by artist and architect André Smith. Small cottages and studios are set around pretty grounds inside a walled garden, with murals, sculptures, and bas reliefs inspired by Aztec/Mayan designs. It offers galleries, workshops, concerts, and events.

Maitland Historical Museum and Telephone Museum

Next door is the **Maitland Historical Museum and Telephone Museum** ❹ (221 W Packwood Avenue; tel: 407-644-1364; www.maitlandhistory.org; Tue–Sun 11am–4pm). The former has exhibits on the early days of the town and regional history, set in a quaint house. Behind it, the Telephone Museum has a collection of early phones and memorabilia.

Waterhouse Residence Museum and Carpentry Shop Museum

Turn right on Maitland Avenue and follow it for two blocks to the shores of Lake Lily, a small, pretty lake teeming with birdlife. You'll see heron, egrets, Muscovy ducks, turtles, and possibly

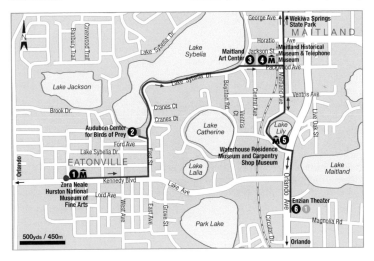

Waiting in line at the Enzian

even alligators along the shore. Follow the path around the lake to visit the **Waterhouse Residence Museum and Carpentry Shop Museum ❺** (840 Lake Lily Drive; tel: 407-644-2451; http://artandhistory.org; Tue–Sun 11am–4pm), which give a glimpse of the lifestyle of a middle-class pioneer family in the 1880s.

Enzian

If you're visiting Maitland at the end of the day and fancy an unusual evening out, turn right out of the parking area onto Orlando Avenue and drive a few blocks south to Magnolia Road where you'll find the **Enzian ❻**, see ❶, (1300 S Orlando Avenue; tel: 407-629-0054; www.enzian.org; hours and admission vary). At this alternative movie theater you can have a drink and a meal while watching first-run independent features.

WEKIWA SPRINGS STATE PARK

To continue north, take Maitland Avenue north to Maitland Boulevard and turn left, which leads back to I-4 – take exit 94. Turn left (west) on Route 434 and then right on Wekiwa Springs Road. This brings you to the entrance of **Wekiwa Springs State Park ❼** (1800 Wekiwa Circle, Apopka; tel: 407-884-2008; www.floridastateparks.org/wekiwasprings; daily 8am–sunset).

With enormous oak and cypress trees, this beautiful 7,800-acre (3,160-hectare) park, just 20 minutes north of the city, is a favorite getaway for Orlando residents. You can swim in a natural spring, or rent canoes to paddle along the Wekiwa River and Rock Springs Run. There are also hiking and biking trails.

LAKE JESSUP

Alternatively, to travel the central Florida waters at a faster pace, turn right on Route 434 from the interstate and head east to Lake Jessup. Turn left on DeLeon Street, then left on Howard Avenue. This curves towards the lake and becomes Black Hammock Road, then Black Hammock Fish Camp Road. Park at the marina.

A 30-minute airboat ride with **Black Hammock Airboat Adventure ❽** (2356

Wekiwa Springs *Manatees at Blue Springs State Park*

Black Hammock Fish Camp Road, Oviedo; tel: 407-977-8235; www.blackhammock airboatrides.com; daily 9.30am–5.30pm) is a great way to explore this lake on the edge of what is often called the Central Florida Everglades. The lake is home to bald eagles, a host of birdlife, bobcats, turtles, and more than 10,000 alligators. If you don't spot one, you can see them in the live gator exhibit. Afterwards enjoy the views from the **Lazy Gator Bar and Black Hammock Restaurant**, see ➋.

BLUE SPRINGS STATE PARK

In the winter, a rare chance to see manatees in the wild awaits further north at **Blue Springs State Park** ➒ (2100 W French Avenue, Orange City; tel: 386-775-3663; www.floridastateparks.org/park/Blue-Spring; daily 8am–sunset). From I-4, take exit 104 and follow US 17/92 to Orange City. Turn west on French Avenue and follow it until the pavement ends; turn left for the park entrance.

Set along the St. Johns River, this beautiful park contains large natural springs which are a winter refuge for the manatee. The manatees swim upriver from November to March to shelter in the warm waters; February is the top viewing month. A boardwalk with viewing platforms runs along the springs, and on a good day you can see dozens of these giant, gentle creatures submerged just below the clear surface.

During the summer when the manatees have gone, you can swim, snorkel, and tube in the springs. You can also rent canoes and kayaks, and there are picnic areas, campsites, and hiking trails. The **Louis Thursby House**, former home of a pioneer citrus grower, is open Wednesday to Sunday. Thursby's Blue Spring Landing, once a busy port for paddle wheelers, is now the departure point for St. Johns River Cruises (tel: 386-917-0724; www.sjrivercruises.com), which offer two-hour nature cruises through this remarkable ecosystem.

Food and drink

➊ ENZIAN

1300 S Orlando Avenue; tel: 407-629-0054; $

Choose from a tasty menu of sandwiches, pizza, pasta, salads, shared plates, and desserts, and there is a selection of wines and beers as well as coffees and organic teas.

➋ LAZY GATOR BAR AND BLACK HAMMOCK RESTAURANT

2356 Black Hammock Fish Camp Road, Oviedo; tel: 407-977-8235; $–$$

The full-menu restaurant serves gator bites, catfish, and Florida seafood favorites. Two lakeside bars have live entertainment on Friday and Saturday nights and Sunday afternoons.

Witnessing a launch

THE SPACE COAST

Many visitors make a daytrip to the Kennedy Space Center, an hour+ drive from Orlando. But with a superb wildlife refuge, pristine national seashore, and the attractions of Cocoa Beach, the Space Coast is well worth further exploration.

DISTANCE: 180 miles (290km)
TIME: One to two days
START: Orlando
END: Cocoa Village
POINTS TO NOTE: Be aware that the Space Coast's attractions are spread out. A stay in the surf capital of Cocoa Beach for a night or two is recommended to take in the area's other highlights.

The Atlantic shores of Florida's Space Coast are the closest beaches to Orlando. Spread along barrier islands, they are connected to the mainland by causeways across the broad Indian and Banana rivers.

KENNEDY SPACE CENTER

Leave Orlando on Toll Road 528, known as the Beachline Expressway (or Bee-line Expressway, an older name). Turn left (north) on SR 407 and right (east) on SR405, which leads to the **Kennedy Space Center Visitor Complex ❶**

(State Road 405, Merritt Island; tel: 855-433-4210; www.kennedyspacecenter.com; daily from 9am).

Although at first glance it appears small compared to the theme parks, even with a full day you'll be hard pressed to fit everything in. In addition to the Visitor Complex, a main component is the bus tour that takes you to assorted outlying sites. This alone takes around three hours, as much time is spent getting on and off the buses and lining up for the next leg of the tour. A daily schedule that gives starting times for the various films and attractions is included with your map of the complex.

For an extra dose of education, rent a KSC Smartguide for the day. It provides maps, a customized audio tour, and fun facts in eight languages. If you're carrying a smartphone, you can also upgrade to the Space Visor, which provides virtual tours of restricted areas.

Additional tours are available for a fee; click the Add On Enhancements and Packages buttons on the Tickets & Packages webpage or ask at the ticket booth. If you want to view a rocket launch, this

Exhibit at the Space Center

The Visitor Complex is fun and informative

is available as an add-on package. Alternatively, you can view the launch from along US Highway 1 North, near Titusville, where you can see the launch pad across the Indian River. Check www.spacecoast launches.com for the schedule.

The Visitor Complex

Walk through the information center to the outdoor plaza. We recommend you make a beeline for the bus tours, as the waits get longer and the sun hotter as the day goes on. Alternatively, explore the Visitor Complex first, which has a range of different buildings, exhibits, and outdoor displays.

Make sure to make the Space Shuttle Atlantis with the Shuttle Launch Experience a priority. This new exhibit, in the far right of the complex, is super interactive with 60 hands-on exhibits. You'll get to see the actual Atlantis shuttle, take an 8.5-minute simulated ride that feels as if you're aboard, and be entertained by short films made by astronauts.

If you'd prefer to go in order, look to the left of the entrance for Heroes

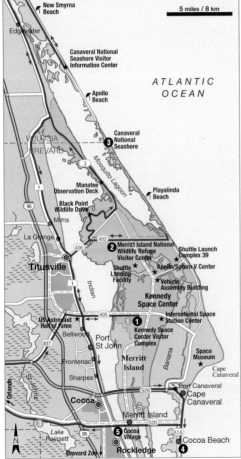

The Rocket Garden impresses at sunset

& Legends, featuring the US Astronaut Hall of Fame. This three-part interactive exhibit uses cutting-edge technology to delve deep into astronauts' experiences. Nearby is the Rocket Garden, a low-tech collection with an impressive array of historic rockets from early space missions. Try and catch one of the fascinating 15-minute guided tours.

Another highlight is the Astronaut Encounter area, where you can meet an astronaut who has flown into space; for an additional fee you can actually have **Lunch with an Astronaut**, see ●. At Journey to Mars: Explorers Wanted, multimedia-based exhibits enlighten visitors about past and current Mars-related events. In the building behind, the IMAX 3D space films are interesting, too. Towards the back of the complex, the dramatic Space Mirror Memorial honors 24 astronauts who died in service on three missions.

Space Center tours

Turn right at the entrance to reach the pick-up point for the KSC bus tour. The drivers give a running commentary, and point out the resident wildlife.

The restricted areas you'll get to see change periodically, and more than one tour might be available per day, but all are fascinating. A frequent destination is the Vehicle Assembly Building, where rockets are put together; at 525ft (160-meters) tall it is the largest single-story building in the world. You might also be shown the future mobile launcher of NASA's Space Launch System and the Launch Control Center, which controlled all space-shuttle launches. The Apollo/Saturn V Center allows you to walk around and under a fully restored Saturn V moon rocket, as well as showing a fascinating multimedia recreation of the first Saturn V manned mission launch.

MERRITT ISLAND WILDLIFE

There is no public access beyond the Space Center Visitor Complex, so you must drive back across the SR 405 causeway and north on US 1 through Titusville to reach the **Merritt Island National Wildlife Refuge** ❷ (tel: 321-861-0667; www.fws.gov/merrittisland; open sunrise–sunset). It is signposted from town – take SR 406/402 (Garden

Space Center wildlife

Only about 10 percent of the Kennedy Space Center's 140,000 acres (34,000 hectares) is used for the space program. The rest is a designated nature reserve. On the KSC bus tour, keep an eye out for alligators sunning beside the ponds. You may also see some of the reserve's 10,000 wild pigs. Drivers will point out enormous eagle's nests; there are now 16 nests in the reserve, some measuring 7ft (2 meters) wide and weighing around 1,000 pounds (450kg).

US Astronaut Hall of Fame   *Merritt Island National Wildlife Refuge*

Street). If you are coming from I-95 take exit 220.

Start at the **Visitor Center** (Nov–Mar daily 9am–4pm, Apr–Oct Mon–Sat 9am–4pm), where you can pick up maps and information about the wildlife, walking trails, and drives in the reserve. Some 43 miles (69km) long, the island is the habitat for over 500 wildlife species, many of which are threatened or endangered. In addition to osprey, bald eagles, heron, egrets, and pelicans, you may see alligators, raccoons, wild hogs and river otters.

Highly recommended is the Black Point Wildlife Drive, a 7-mile (11km) self-guided auto tour through one of the best wildlife-viewing areas, with information on 12 numbered stops. Just before stop 11, watch for the large alligator often seen sunning him- (her-?) self on the right side of the road.

Another highlight is the Manatee Observation Deck beside the Haulover Canal on SR 3. Manatees thrive here year-round, thanks to a ban on motorized vessels in the surrounding area; they are most frequently seen in spring and autumn.

CANAVERAL NATIONAL SEASHORE

Adjacent to the wildlife refuge is the **Canaveral National Seashore ❸** (tel: 321-267-1110; www.nps.gov/CANA). At the southern end, lovely Playalinda Beach is accessible via SR 402 through the reserve. To reach Apollo Beach at the northern end, drive north on SR 3 and US 1 to SR A1A, where you'll also find the visitor center, walking trails, and other facilities. In between are miles of beautiful, undeveloped stretches of beach backed by barrier dunes and the Mosquito Lagoon. This area provides a haven for loggerhead turtles, fish, and shellfish, waterfowl, migrating birds and, of course, human beachcombers.

COCOA BEACH

Take US Highway 1 south and turn left (east) on SR 528. After passing Cape Canaveral and Port Canaveral, with its busy cruise terminal, the road curves south towards **Cocoa Beach ❹**. Known as Florida's surf capital, it has long stretches of broad sandy beach, a laid-back, youthful vibe, and a string of upbeat, barefoot-casual restaurants and bars.

The town's landmark is the **Westgate Cocoa Beach Pier**, which juts 800 feet (245 meters) out above the ocean from Meade Avenue. The arcade atop its rustic wooden pylons is lined with restaurants, bars, shops, and a fishing deck, with lifeguards on duty. Right at the end of the pier, **Rikki Tiki Tavern**, see ❷, offers seafood, cocktails and panoramic ocean views.

On the corner of SR 520 and Atlantic Avenue you'll find the 'one of a kind' **Ron Jon Surf Shop** (888-757-8737; www.

Cocoa Beach bathed in sunshine

ronjonsurfshop.com; open 24 hours), a temple to the glorified beach lifestyle filled with surf clothes, accessories, and boards of every size and style. Next door is the **Cocoa Beach Surf Company Surf Complex** (321-799-9930; www.cocoa beachsurf.com), selling more beach gear and with its own shark-filled aquarium. The Shark Pit Bar & Grill, see page 119, is a relaxing bar and restaurant inside the retail emporium.

Take SR 520 across three causeways to the west side of the Indian River. Turn left on Brevard Avenue to reach **Cocoa Village ⑤**, an artsy enclave of historic buildings that now house galleries, antiques shops, boutiques, and specialty stores.

Continue west on SR 520. Four miles (6km) past the junction of I-95, before you cross the St Johns River, look out on your left for the **Lone Cabbage Fish Camp**, see ③. This rustic roadhouse-style bar and restaurant is a popular place for airboat rides along the river, spotting alligators and other wildlife.

Beyond the bridge, SR 520 curves north to intersect with SR 528 which will take you back to Orlando.

Brevard Zoo

If you have extra time, visit the **Brevard Zoo** (8225 N Wickham Road, Melbourne; 321-254-9453; www.brevardzoo.org; daily 9:30am–5pm). To get there from Cocoa Beach Pier, drive south down A1A for about 10 minutes, then turn east on Pineda Causeway to US 1. Go north on US 1 and then turn left onto Suntree Boulevard, right onto North Wickham Road, and follow the signs. Home to more than 800 animals, this zoo has a bonus: active travelers can opt to kayak around the animals or go zip-lining over them.

Food and drink

① LUNCH WITH AN ASTRONAUT
Kennedy Space Center Visitor Complex; tel: 321-449-4400; $$
After a buffet lunch, an astronaut presents an entertaining and informative talk on his or her experiences in space, answers questions, and signs autographs. Book ahead as places are limited.

② RIKKI TIKI TAVERN
Cocoa Beach Pier; www.cocoabeachpier. com/dining/rikki-tiki-tavern; $
Enjoy a drink, bites and splendid ocean views from the end of the Cocoa Beach Pier. The pier has four additional restaurants.

③ LONE CABBAGE FISH CAMP
SR 520 at St Johns River; tel: 321-632-4199; www.twisterairboatrides.com/ fishcamp.html; $
Try alligator tail, turtle, catfish, and other local favorites at this rustic riverside bar and restaurant. Live music on Sunday afternoons.

Canoeing up the Hillsborough River

TAMPA BAY

Another great theme park, Busch Gardens, draws many visitors to Tampa Bay. But with beautiful Gulf Coast beaches, good museums, a scenic river and Riverwalk, the Florida Aquarium, and a historic district to explore, there are plenty of reasons to extend your stay.

DISTANCE: 120 miles (190km)
TIME: One to three days
START: Orlando
END: Fort De Soto Park
POINTS TO NOTE: Traffic can be heavy in the metro area, especially on I-275 across Tampa Bay, so allow extra time to arrive at your destination.

With its busy port and downtown business district, the city of Tampa is the commercial center of Florida's Gulf coast. Across Tampa Bay lie St Petersburg and Clearwater, the largest of the communities covering the Pinellas Peninsula, with a string of barrier-island beaches along the Gulf of Mexico. Together they form one of Florida's largest metropolitan areas with a population rivaling Miami's, but on the whole the bay area maintains a relaxed, casual atmosphere.

Tampa is only an hour+ drive from Orlando (avoid rush hour), and even if you only have a day to spare, an excursion here gives you plenty of variety and a chance to see this vibrant Gulf Coast region. Many cultural institutions are situated along the new 2.4-mile (4 km) Tampa Riverwalk (www.thetampariverwalk.com), a pedestrian pathway that also links to parks, restaurants, historical monuments, and hotels.

This route takes in some of the highlights of Tampa Bay, from Tampa's northeast corner, downtown to Ybor City, across the bay to St Petersburg, and on to Fort De Soto Park, with one of the country's most beautiful beaches.

CANOE ESCAPE

The Hillsborough River runs 54 miles (87km) from Green Swamp to Tampa Bay. Fed by pure water from Crystal Springs, it provides around 75 percent of the city's drinking water. Some 20 miles (32km) of the river are protected in a wilderness park, providing a rich habitat for migrating birds and local wildlife. It's one of the best wildlife viewing spots in all of Florida. The ideal way to see it is from the river itself, on a canoe or kayak trip with **Canoe Escape** ❶ (12702 US 301, Thonotosassa, FL

Kumba's many loops

33592; tel: 813-986-2067; www.canoe escape.com; daily 9am–5pm).

From Orlando, take I-4 West to I-75 (exit 9). Go north on I-75 to Fowler Avenue (exit 265). Exit to your right (east) until it dead-ends into US 301. Turn left and drive 3.5 miles (5.6km). Turn into John B. Sargeant Park on the left-hand side. Canoe Escape is located within the park.

Most trips are self-guided and range from 4.5 miles (7km; 2 hours) to 9 miles (14km; 4 hours). There is a longer trip for seasoned paddlers. Transportation and orientation is provided. Interpretive guided trips with an experienced chaperon are also available.

This peaceful and scenic river, lined with cypress, oaks, and thick woodlands, truly is an escape from the busy cities and theme parks. Paddling here is gentle and relaxed, yet there's a real sense of adventure as you glide along the banks, looking for wildlife. Two of the top birds to see are limpkins and Roseate spoonbills, both prominent in Central and South America and at the top of their range here in Florida. Depending on conditions and the season, you may see alligators, turtles, wild pigs, raccoons, and a variety of herons, egrets, hawks, woodpeckers, kingfishers, wood storks, and anhingas.

BUSCH GARDENS TAMPA BAY

Wildlife of a larger variety can be seen 2 miles (3km) west of I-75 (exit 54) at **Busch Gardens Tampa Bay ❷** (10165 N McKinley Drive, Tampa; tel: 813-884-4386; www.buschgardenstampa.com; daily 10pm–6pm, but check website for changes). This popular theme park combines spectacular thrill rides and live shows with one of North America's largest zoos. If you don't want to drive from Orlando, consider taking the Busch Gardens Shuttle Express (tel: 800-221-1339), which provides free round-trip transportation from several Orlando locations.

More than 12,000 exotic animals, including several endangered species, live in natural habitats resembling those of their native Africa. The largest is the 65-acre (26-hectare) Serengeti Plain, where zebras, giraffes, black rhinos, impalas, and other wild animals roam freely. You can view them from a train that goes around the plain or from the Skyride that goes over it. For a closer encounter, take the Serengeti Safari, a half-hour, off-road ride in a flatbed truck across the middle of the reserve. You'll stop and hand-feed giraffes along the way.

Walk along the Edge of Africa for a look at lions, lemurs, crocodiles, and hippos swimming in their pool. Other highlights are the Myombe Reserve and Jungala, where you can see gorillas, chimpanzees, and tigers.

Busch Gardens contains some of the region's most awesome thrill rides. Falcon's Fury, North America's tallest freestanding drop tower, looms at 335ft (102 meters) and takes riders soaring straight down at 60mph (97kph).

Rhinos at Busch Gardens

Falcon's Fury drops 335ft (102 meters)

SheiKra is a dive coaster that moves you 200ft (60 meters) up, then 90 degrees straight down in a floorless car going 70mph (110 kph). More death-defying loops, dives, drops, and inversions are in store on the Kumba and Montu roller coasters at opposite ends of the park. The park's newest attraction, the Cobra's Curse coaster, puts a spin on family thrills with a 70ft (21-meter) vertical lift that brings you face-to-face with an 80ft (25-meter) snake king's fangs.

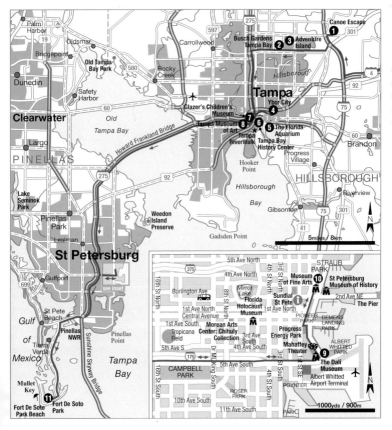

Younger visitors enjoying The Florida Aquarium

ADVENTURE ISLAND

Across the street, **Adventure Island** (10001 N McKinley Drive, Tampa; tel: 888-800-5447; https://adventureisland.com/en/tampa; hours vary by season) is a 30-acre (12-hectare) water park with a Key West theme and a combination of calm and thrilling water experiences.

YBOR CITY

Take Busch Boulevard west to I-275, and take it south to downtown Tampa and **Ybor City** (www.ybormuseum.org), one of the bay area's most historic districts. This is Tampa's Latin Quarter, founded in 1886 when Vicente Martinez Ybor moved his cigar-manufacturing business here from Key West. At one time Ybor City had 200 cigar factories, with hundreds of workers in each one. Master cigar craftsmen and workers from Cuba, Spain, and Italy came and made their homes in this vibrant multicultural neighborhood, also rich with German and Eastern European immigrants. The original immigrants' backyard chickens have evolved into the current population of wild ones.

The red-brick buildings, wrought-iron balconies, and brick-lined streets survive, making it one of the most charming areas of the city. The cigar shops, still prominent here, have been joined by trendy shops and vintage-clothing boutiques. After dark, Ybor City is Tampa's liveliest nightlife area.

The heart of the district along 7th Avenue – La Setima – is lined with bars, clubs, restaurants, cafés, and cigar bars, which come into their own after 5pm. **Centro Ybor**, see , has several good bars and cafés. Further along 7th Avenue is the beautiful tiled facade of the **Columbia Restaurant**, see , a local institution.

A Saturday market (www.ybormarket.com) takes place in Centennial Park at 9th Avenue and 19th Street. Opposite is the **Ybor City Museum State Park** (1818 9th Avenue; tel: 813-247-6323; www.ybormuseum.org; Wed–Sun 9am–5pm), set in an old bakery dating from 1896. Here you can watch some of the last of the master cigar rollers at work, and take a walking tour of the district. Next door, several small cottages, or *casitas*, where the workers once lived provide a truly fascinating look into the life of the community.

THE FLORIDA AQUARIUM

From Ybor City, take 13th Street south toward the port, where it becomes Channelside Drive. Follow signs for **The Florida Aquarium** (701 Channelside Drive; tel: 813-273-4000; www.flaquarium.org; daily 9.30am–5pm), home to more than 20,000 plants and animals from around the world.

Starting on the upper level, the exhibit pathway follows a drop of rain on its journey to the depths of the ocean, passing through a variety of watery habitats

Ybor City lights up in the evening

beginning with Florida's wetlands, where you'll see playful river otters and free-flying birds. You can also get up-close views of ring-tailed lemurs and an Indian Ocean coral reef in the aquarium's newest exhibit – Journey to Madagascar. Other highlights include views of sand tiger sharks, sea turtles, and thousands of tropical fish in a coral-reef environment that is a partial replica of the Dry Tortugas in Key West.

This excellent aquarium has numerous shows and demonstrations throughout the day that both educate and entertain, and features up-close encounters, behind-the-scenes tours, in-water guest experiences, and even a Wild Dolphin cruise on Tampa Bay. There is an on-site café, and a new outdoor recreational area features a splash pad, outdoor bar, and 4-D theater.

TAMPA BAY HISTORY CENTER

Continue along Channelside Drive to the start of **Tampa Riverwalk**, a landscaped trail along the waterfont with several sculptures, memorials, parks, restaurants, and other places of interest. The next few sights are located along the Riverwalk, so you can take a break from driving.

Learn about Tampa's Native American residents, its pirates, and current-day favorites – like its Buccaneers football team – at the growing **Tampa Bay History Center** ❻ (801 Old Water Street; tel: 813-228-0097; http://tampabay historycenter.org; daily 10am–5pm). Its

impressive map gallery contains nearly 3,000 maps and charts, which provide a visual representation of Florida's history and development over almost 500 years.

GLAZER'S CHILDREN'S MUSEUM

Further along the Tampa Riverwalk is the **Glazer's Children's Museum** ❼ (110

Alternative transport

Tampa Bay's first electric streetcar lines were built in 1892; by 1926 they had become an essential means of transport, with nearly 24-million passengers. But two decades later they were discontinued after World War II. Today, TECO Line trolleys (www.tecolinestreetcar.org) are rolling through the city once again. Public buses 4 and 19 run from Downtown to Hyde Park; the TECO Line streetcar connects Ybor City to these areas. Downtown St Petersburg is served by the Looper Trolley (http://loopertrolley.com), while the Suncoast Beach Trolley (www.psta.net/beachtrolley.php) makes its way along the Gulf Coast. The Downtowner (www.ride downtowner.com/cities/tampa) offers free shuttle rides through an app.

See the area by boat via the bright yellow Pirate Water Taxi line (http://pirate watertaxi.com), offering day passes along the waterfront, or by bicycle. Coast Bike Share (http://coastbikeshare.com) has rental stations throughout downtown Tampa.

Exhibit at the Museum of Fine Arts

W Gasparilla Plaza; tel: 813-443-3861; glazermuseum.org; Mon–Fri 10am–5pm, Sat 10am–6pm, Sun 1–6pm), a big draw for families. More than 170 interactive exhibits in zones ranging from Gadget Garage, with its focus on robotics, to Central Bank, where children learn to earn and save money with simple math, matching and physical activities, give little ones aged 10 and under the chance to play, build, learn, and experiment. They can also climb a rock wall sized just right.

TAMPA MUSEUM OF ART

Continue along the Riverwalk to the **Tampa Museum of Art ❽** (120 W Gasparilla Plaza; tel: 813-274-8130; www.tampamuseum.org; Mon–Thu 11am–

> ## Chihuly glasswork
>
> If you have some extra time in St Petersburg, walk to the multi-part Morean Arts Center, which is best known for the **Chihuly Collection** (720 Central Avenue; tel: 727-822-7872; www.moreanartscenter.org/chihuly), which features a permanent collection of fabulous, unearthly glass creations by artist Dale Chihuly. Admission includes a live glassblowing demonstration at the Morean Glass Studio & Hot Shop, plus visits to the nearby Morean Arts Center and the Morean Center for Clay (located in the Warehouse Arts District), featuring contemporary art by local, regional, and national artists.

7pm, Fri until 10pm, Sun until 5pm). It contains a fine collection of Greek and Roman antiquities, as well as artworks from the 20th century to the present.

THE DALÍ MUSEUM

Arguably the area's most impressive museum lies across Tampa Bay in St Petersburg. You'll need to get back in the car and take I-275 south across the Howard Frankland Bridge. Then take I-175 East (exit 22, on your left) towards Tropicana Field. Merge onto 5th Avenue/South Dali Boulevard until you reach the artfully shaped glass-panelled **Dalí Museum ❾** on the left (1 Dali Boulevard, St Petersburg; tel: 727-823-3767; www.thedali.org; daily 10am–5.30pm, Thu until 8pm); it's the only three-star Michelin-rated museum in the south.

This excellent three-floor museum houses the largest collection of Salvador Dalí's works outside of Spain. Among its 2,000 pieces are eight master works. It is based on the private collection amassed by A. Reynolds Morse, a Cleveland industrialist, and his wife, Eleanor.

The works are displayed on a rotating basis, in changing exhibitions that also incorporate works on loan from top collections around the world. Take a free docent or audio tour for a fascinating insight into the artist and his works. The gift shop has an exceptional collection of art-related items, 85 percent of them exclusive to the museum, and the Café Gala has Spanish bites.

The renowned Dalí Museum

Idyllic Fort De Soto Park beach

MUSEUM OF FINE ARTS

There is another art museum not to be missed nearby in downtown St Petersburg. Head northeast on Dali Boulevard, which turns into Bayshore Drive SE as you bear left. After a few blocks turn left onto Central Avenue SE, then right onto Beach Drive NE, to reach the **Museum of Fine Arts** ❿ (255 Beach Drive NE; tel: 727-896-2667; http://mfastpete.org; Mon–Wed and Fri–Sat 10am–5pm, Thu 10am–8pm, Sun noon–5pm). Monet, Morisot, Rodin, O'Keeffe, and Willem de Kooning are among the major artists represented here. There is also an outstanding photography collection, as well as displays of pre-Columbian, Native American, African, Egyptian, Asian, and Greek and Roman art.

For a well-deserved meal, head to **Farmtable Kitchen**, see ❸, for Michael Mina's hearty creations.

FORT DE SOTO PARK AND BEACH

You're spoiled for choice with the string of beaches ranging all the way along the barrier islands on the Gulf Coast. For a real gem, however, take I-275 south to the Pinellas Bayway (toll) to reach **Fort De Soto Park** ⓫ (3500 Pinellas Bayway S, Tierra Verde; tel: 727-582-2267; www.fortdesoto.com).

With good swimming and three miles (5km) of pure white sand, Fort De Soto Park beach is regularly named as one of the best beaches in the US. The park contains a historic fort built during the Spanish-American War, fishing piers, campsites, and walking trails through a wild, natural landscape. Visit during the week and you may find you have it largely to yourself.

Food and drink

❶ CENTRO YBOR

8th Avenue between 15th and 17th streets, Ybor City; www.centroybor.com; $
Covering two blocks, this complex has several good bars, including the Tampa Bay Brewing Company, as well as cafés and restaurants for a coffee or quick bite to eat.

❷ COLUMBIA RESTAURANT

2117 E. 7th Avenue, Ybor City; tel: 813-248-4961; $$$
Five generations of the same family have been serving Cuban classics in this personable Ybor City restaurant — the oldest in the state, dating to 1905. It has spawned fancier, less personable clones elsewhere in Central Florida.

❸ FARMTABLE KITCHEN

179 2nd Avenue North, St. Petersburg; tel: 727-523-6297; www.localegourmetmarket.com/farmtable-kitchen; $$–$$$
Creative and grilled foods, plus pizzas, from celebrity chef Michael Mina, served on the top floor of the bi-level gourmet food hall Locale Market.

DIRECTORY

Hand-picked hotels and restaurants to suit all budgets and tastes, organized by area, plus select nightlife listings, an alphabetical listing of practical information, and an overview of the best books and movies to give you a flavor of the city.

Little Mermaid–themed courtyard at the Art of Animation

ACCOMMODATIONS

With more than 460 hotels and 120,000 guestrooms, Orlando has a wealth of lodging options. Accommodations range from luxury resorts and themed hotels to charming bed and breakfasts, economy hotels/motels, and campgrounds. Well over 20,000 vacation homes (21,700 in Osceola County alone) are also available for rental, along with more than 25,000 vacation ownership units. Although standards for services and facilities are generally quite high, there is the occasional bad apple, so be sure you know what you're getting into before signing on the dotted line.

Reservations and prices

Reservations are generally required, and if you are traveling during the high season you should book several months ahead if you have your heart set on a particular hotel or if you want to stay inside Walt Disney World Resort.

Room rates vary enormously between high season and low season. The Christmas break period (mid–December until New Year) is the most expensive, followed by spring break (mid-February until the end of March) and summer (end of May until the beginning of August). The cheapest times to visit are from New Year until mid-February; September after Labor Day (but be prepared for extraordinary heat); and the first half of December, when the weather is perfect.

Don't forget to check the hidden charges when booking a hotel. All hotels add a bed tax, which varies from county to county and can be as high as 13 percent. There is plenty of scope to ask for a discount if you are staying for a week or more, or if you are visiting during the off-season, which for many hotels is a lean time.

Price for a standard double room for one night without breakfast:
$$$ = over US$200
$$ = US$110–200
$ = under US$110

Booking the biggies

Both the Disney World and Universal Orlando complexes offer perks to guests who stay in on-site hotels. Disney offers, among other extras, free bus and sometimes boat transportation, free parking, and extra theme-park hours. Some non-Disney lodging facilities that are located on Disney property offer these perks too. At Universal, on-site guests can expect free shuttles, plus 'Express' access to nearly all rides and attractions, early admission to The Wizarding World of Harry Potter, and priority seating at several restaurants.

Information on all of Disney's resort hotels can be found at www.disney-world.com. Likewise, you can book your

Room at the BoardWalk Inn

stay at Universal Orlando hotels online. Visit Universal's website, www.universalorlando.com, or Loews', https://uo.loewshotels.com.

Theme-park transportation

There is hardly a hotel or motel in central Florida that does not list 'free transportation to Disney' as one of its amenities, but the services most provide are very limited, with one departure and one return from each park per day. The timings are often inconvenient too, meaning you'll miss the quieter morning hours and the evening shows and fireworks. Instead, you may want to rent a car, or hire a taxi, Uber or Lyft vehicle.

Walt Disney World Resort

All-Star Movies, Music, and Sports
1991 West Buena Vista Drive, Lake Buena Vista; tel: 407-939-1936; $
This is one of three budget Disney complexes. It has 30 three-story buildings divided by themes. Each has a distinctive facade, but aside from a few decorative touches, the size and decor of most rooms are identical: they're 260 sq ft (24 sq meters), have two double beds, small bureaus, a table with chairs, and bathrooms with separate vanity areas. The All-Star Music hotel also has family suites that sleep six with two bathrooms and a kitchenette. Popular with families, the resort has a game room, playground, outdoor pool, shopping, and food court.

Art of Animation
1850 Animation Way, Lake Buna Vista; tel: 407-938-7000; $$
This hotel – themed around *Cars*, *Finding Nemo*, *The Little Mermaid*, and *The Lion King* – is considered a value resort even though rates are a bit higher. For the extra money, you get a cleverly designed suite that sleeps six, with ingenious RV-like tricks such as beds hidden in tables, plus two bathrooms and a kitchenette — way less costly than two rooms.

B Resort & Spa
1905 Hotel Plaza Boulevard, Lake Buena Vista; tel: 866-759-9832; www.bhotelsandresorts.com/b-resort-and-spa; $$
Mixing form with function, this chic hotel, located on Disney property but owned by a different company, has high style and low prices – plus Disney perks like free theme-park shuttles. With a pool, bunk-bed options, and an Aveda spa, you'll have everything you need.

Boardwalk Inn and Villas
2101 Epcot Resorts Boulevard, Lake Buena Vista; tel: 407-939-6200; $$$
Elaborately detailed buildings with turreted, brightly colored facades and twinkling lights that recreate an East Coast boardwalk circa 1920. Spacious rooms with appropriate theming have extra comforts; the two-story garden suites have private gardens. The villas – Disney Vacation Club units – sleep

The Villas are the most recent addition to the Grand Floridian Resort & Spa

4 to 12 and have kitchens, laundries, and whirlpool tubs. Nightclubs, restaurants, midway games, and shops line the boardwalk, which also has free family-friendly entertainment nightly. There's a supervised evening children's program, a health club, a large swimming pool with a 200-ft (60-meter) water slide, and boat transportation to Epcot and Disney's Hollywood Studios.

Fort Wilderness Resort

4510 N Fort Wilderness Trai, Lake Buena Vista; tel: 407-824-2000; $–$$

Fort Wilderness Resort has more than 800 campsites for tents and RVs. Another option is to rent a Wilderness Cabin that sleeps up to six people and has air conditioning, color TV, radio, cookware, and linen. The resort is located amid 700 acres (283 hectares) of woods and streams on Bay Lake, east of the Magic Kingdom.

Four Seasons Orlando at Walt Disney World Resort

10100 Dream Tree Boulevard, Lake Buena Vista; tel: 407-313-6868; www.fourseasons. com/orlando; $$$

Golden Oak is a new luxury residential neighborhood on Disney World property, and a 443-room Four Seasons hotel beckons behind its guarded gates. Excellence is a basic here. A rooftop Spanish steakhouse, Capa, has an expansive open-air lounge offering seemingly unlimited views of Disney World. Also on property are a golf clubhouse, tennis courts, a water park, an adults-only pool, and a spa.

Grand Floridian Resort & Spa

4401 Grand Floridian Way, Lake Buena Vista; tel: 407-939-1936; $$$

The Victorian era in all its splendor is recreated at Disney's flagship property, an elegant confection of glistening white, wooden buildings with red-shingled roofs, gracious verandas, and turrets. Most rooms in the four- and five-story lodge buildings have two queen-size beds and a daybed; many overlook the Seven Seas Lagoon. Amenities include some of Disney's finest dining experiences; several bars; a supervised children's evening program; Senses Spa; three swimming pools; and water activities. Monorail to Epcot and Magic Kingdom, boat to Magic Kingdom. The Villas addition has studio and one- and two-bedroom Vacation Club lodgings.

The Grove Resort & Spa

14501 Grove Resort Avenue, Orlando; tel: 407-545-7500; www.groveresortorlando. com; $$

Undeveloped land on the western side of Disney World is becoming a small, quiet hotel destination, and The Grove offers an all-suite experience on Lake Austin. The 106-acre (43-hectare) property, opening in stages, will ultimately have 878 suites as well as three pools, restaurants and bars, a spa, a watersports pier, and a water park with a surf simulator.

Italianate Loews Portofino Bay Hotel

Polynesian Village Resort

1600 Seven Seas Drive,
Lake Buena Vista; tel: 407-824-2000;
$$$

One of Disney's most authentic theme hotels recreates a Pacific Island retreat. The centerpiece is the Great Ceremonial House, a tropical extravaganza of plants and waterfalls. Rooms, in 11 two- and three-story 'longhouses', vary in size, but most have two queen-size beds, a daybed, and balconies. Those overlooking the Seven Seas Lagoon afford front-row seats for Magic Kingdom fireworks. There are several restaurants and bars, two pools, a playground, supervised evening children's programs, and water activities. The over-the-water bungalows, part of Disney Vacation Club, bring Pacific Island-style luxury to those with the budget to rent them. Monorail to Magic Kingdom and Epcot; boat to Magic Kingdom.

Universal Orlando Resort

Cabana Bay Beach Resort

6550 Adventure Way, Orlando; tel: 407-503-4000; $$

Universal's sole value-priced resort, Cabana Bay recently expanded to comprise 2,200 guest rooms and suites – some sleeping six with pull-out sofas. The wholesome retro 1950s-60s theme is the backdrop for amenities including two zero-entry pools, a lazy river, and a 10-lane bowling alley. Early admission to the Wizarding World of Harry Potter is included.

Hard Rock Hotel

5800 Universal Boulevard, Orlando; tel: 407-503-2000; www.hardrockhotels.com/orlando; $$$

The accommodations at this Mission-style hotel range from very comfortable standard rooms to large and opulent suites. Just ask, and the staff will deliver a guitar or DJ mixer to your room so you can tinker all you want. It's part of the Sound of Your Stay program, which also includes music downloads. An eclectic array of rock 'n' roll memorabilia is displayed tastefully around the building, which nearly surrounds a huge pool with a sandy beach, water slide, and underwater sound system. Several restaurants and bars, a fitness room, an indoor play area, and a Hard Rock store complete the picture.

Loews Portofino Bay Hotel

5601 Universal Boulevard, Orlando; tel: 407-503-1000; $$$

This is such a beautifully designed and constructed recreation of the real Portofino, you'd be forgiven for calling out *buon giorno* from your window first thing in the morning, especially after that first cup of stiff Italian coffee. Set on a harbor filled with fishing boats, the hotel offers some of the most luxurious accommodations in Orlando, with large, sumptuous rooms, three elaborate pools, a spa, an indoor children's play area, and several restaurants, including a local branch of the international Italian chain BiCE. Very expensive, but worth it.

Rooms have a tropical vibe at the Loews Sapphire Falls Resort

Loews Sapphire Falls Resort

6601 Adventure Way, Orlando; tel: 888-273-1311; $$

With a cheerful Caribbean theme, Loews Sapphire Falls Resort has a tropical island feel. Complementing the 1,000 rooms and suites are a pool surrounded by waterfalls, two sand beaches, a fire pit, and two restaurants – one with 75 types of rum. Guests receive special privileges at the Universal Orlando theme parks.

Downtown Orlando

Eö Inn

227 N Eola Drive, Orlando; tel: 407-481-8485; www.eoinn.com; $$$

This historic inn was built in 1923 and overlooks Lake Eola in the prestigious Thornton Park area. It was converted into a fine boutique hotel in 1999. With only 21 rooms, the service is always personable, and the decor is chic and spacious.

Grand Bohemian Hotel Orlando

325 South Orange Avenue, Orlando; tel: 407-313-9000 or 1-866-663-0024; www.grandbohemianhotel.com; $$$

This high-style hotel, across from City Hall, is itself a masterpiece, with more than 1000 pieces of art, including works by Gustav Klimt and Egon Schiele. The Bösendorfer Lounge offers nightly entertainment on one of only two Imperial Grand Bösendorfer pianos in the world. The 247 guest rooms and suites are dramatically furnished in dark Java wood tones, soft red-and-purple velvet fabrics, silver paint, Tiffany-style lamps, and the luxurious all-white 'heavenly bed'. Amenities include a fine restaurant, heated outdoor rooftop pool, spa, massage room, and workout room.

International Drive

Castle Hotel

8629 International Drive, Orlando; tel: 407-345-1511; www.castlehotel orlando.com; $$

Spires, mosaics, and rich purple-and-gold drapes give this mid-range hotel – part of the Marriott Autograph Collection – a touch of medieval whimsy. Amenities include the airy Garden Bistro & Bar, a spa, a lounge, a pleasant heated courtyard pool, two sky terraces, and theme-park shuttles.

The Enclave Hotel & Suites

6165 Carrier Drive, Orlando; tel: 800-457-0077; www.enclavesuites.com; $$

Located just off International Drive, this hotel offers a lot more than the average chain. All the suites include a fully fitted kitchen, and the KidsQuarters suites sleep six in two bedrooms. There are two outdoor pools, one indoor pool, two kiddie pools, a tennis court, a game room, and a playground to keep everyone busy. A food court offers meals and complimentary daily grab-and-go breakfasts.

Rosen Shingle Creek

9939 Universal Boulevard, Orlando;

Rosen Shingle Creek, set in sprawling grounds

tel: 407-996-9939 or 1-866-996-9939; www.rosenshinglecreek.com; $$–$$$

You could almost forget that this gorgeous 1,501-room hotel is right in the heart of Orlando just a mile (1.5km) from the Convention Center. Set back from the main roads on 250 acres (101 hectares), it has an 18-hole championship golf course (recently redesigned by the Arnold Palmer Design Company); tennis courts; a lap pool, zero-entry family pool, and quiet pool with private cabanas surrounded by pretty gardens; and a nature trail alongside cypress-lined Shingle Creek. And there are 15 restaurants and bars to choose from, including A Land Remembered steakhouse (see page 115).

(see page 115).

Kissimmee and Celebration

All Star Vacation Homes

7822 West Irlo Bronson Memorial Highway (Hwy 192), Kissimmee; tel: 407-997-0733; www.allstarvacationhomes.com; $

This leading property management company has more than 275 fully furnished vacation home rentals within 3 to 14 miles (9 to 23km) of Walt Disney World, ranging from two and three-bedroom condos to fabulous 14-bedroom town homes with private pools. Other amenities include spas, game rooms, home movie theaters, and TVs in every bedroom. The homes are beautifully decorated, well-located and maintained, and a great alternative to traditional hotels, especially for longer stays.

Holiday Inn Orlando SW

5711 West US Hwy 192, Kissimmee; tel: 407-396-4222; www.hicelebration. com; $

Across the road from Old Town/Fun Spot and just 3 miles (2km) from Disney, this spacious hotel offers many family facilities and great value. Its 444 rooms are decorated in sophisticated earthy tones, and have private balconies. Amenities include a large outdoor heated pool, separate kids' pool, free meals for children under 12, and complimentary theme-park shuttle transportation.

Reunion Resort

7593 Gathering Drive, Kissimmee; tel: 407-662-1000; www.reunion resort.com; $$$

With three signature golf courses designed by leading golf pros plus a tennis center, spa, water park, and biking and walking trails, this upscale luxury resort has something for every member of the family. It covers 2,300 acres (930 hectares) in a burgeoning area 6 miles (9.5km) south of Walt Disney World. Accommodations range from luxury suites and condos to villas overlooking the golf course to private four to 12-bedroom homes.

Lakeland/Winter Haven

LEGOLAND Beach Retreat

1 Legoland Way, Lakeland; tel: 877-350-5346; www.legoland.com/florida/legoland-beach-retreat/overview/; $$

This new bungalow-style 166-unit hotel groups its accommodations into 13 themed areas, each with its own play area that is visible from the personal patios (so parents can lounge while supervising). Also on offer: a drive-through check-in service, private family villas with bunk and trundle beds to sleep five, a restaurant, a bar, and a LEGO play area.

LEGOLAND Hotel

1 Legoland Way, Winter Haven; 877-350-5346; www.legoland.com/florida/legoland-hotel/overview; $$

If you can't get enough of LEGO, be sure to spend at least a night in this thoroughly LEGO-saturated hotel, where the exterior, room decor, play areas, and location ('150 kid steps' from the LEGOLAND theme park) offer total immersion. LEGO models, LEGO luggage carts, and a LEGO castle are among the lobby extras. An impressive cafeteria and a bar – flagged by LEGO servers – are part of the fun.

Terrace Hotel

329 East Main Street, Lakeland; tel: 863-688-0800; www.terracehotel.com; $$$

This luxury hotel in pretty downtown Lakeland is a good place to stop after a visit to LEGOLAND or en route to Tampa Bay, and makes a nice change from the busier cities without costing you an arm and a leg. Built in the 1920s, it retains lovely period architecture in the Terrace Grille restaurant, with high French windows overlooking Lake Mirror. The 73 rooms are stylishly decorated with beautiful old-fashioned furnishings.

Winter Park and Maitland

The Alfond Inn

300 E New England Avenue, Winter Park; tel: 407-998-8090; www.thealfondinn.com; $$$

Pretty Rollins College's 112-room boutique hotel opened in 2013. This tasteful, pet-friendly lodging facility near the heart of Winter Park has an extensive art collection with 240+ works, plus comfortable rooms, a lovely bar and a nice farm-to-table restaurant with indoor and outdoor seating.

Park Plaza Hotel

307 Park Avenue South, Winter Park; tel: 407-647-1072 or 1-800-228-7220; www.parkplazahotel.com; $$–$$$

From its wood-paneled lobby to the wicker armchairs on the fern-filled, wrought-iron balconies overlooking Park Avenue, this boutique hotel exudes old-fashioned charm. Built in 1921, it is a landmark in the heart of Winter Park's main shopping and dining area. Antiques grace the lobby and guestrooms, where wooden floors, ceiling fans, and different beds in every room add to the ambience.

Thurston House Bed and Breakfast

851 Lake Avenue, Maitland; tel: 407-539-

1911; www.thurstonhouse.com; $$$

Set on the shores of Lake Eulalia, this pretty Victorian farmhouse is a reminder of days long gone in central Florida. One thing that hasn't changed is the fact that you can still sit in a rocking chair on the veranda and watch the osprey dive for fish in the lake. Built in 1885 and restored in 1991, this bed and breakfast combines all the charm of a Victorian inn with the modern amenities you would expect in a small hotel.

The Space Coast

Anthony's on the Beach

3499 S Atlantic Avenue, Cocoa Beach; tel: 321-784-8829; www.anthonysonthe beach.com; $

Cocoa Beach is lined with amenities-rich high-rise hotels, but if you want a real sand-and-surf feel, opt instead for this non-smoking motel that has been around since 1958. Rooms are modest, but priced accordingly.

The Inn at Cocoa Beach

4300 Ocean Beach Boulevard, Cocoa Beach; tel: 800-343-5307; www.theinnat cocoabeach.com; $$–$$$

Gracious and welcoming, this pretty oceanside hotel is a perfect combination of old-fashioned Southern charm and laid-back beach lifestyle. Rooms are individually and tastefully decorated, some with four-poster beds, Jacuzzis, or French country furniture. All have ocean views. The beach is just through the garden gate, and there's even a colorful parrot for company.

Tampa Bay

Epicurean

1207 S Howard Avenue, Tampa; tel: 813-999-8700; http://epicureanhotel.com; $$$

True to its name, food and wine are at the heart of this hotel. You'll be greeted with a sip of wine at the crate-themed check-in area, dine in a restaurant with hydroponic herbs growing from the wall, and find fine wines in each guestroom. From spa treatments using edible greens to pool floats resembling citrus slices, this stylish hotel is a dream for the culinarily inclined.

Seminole Hard Rock Hotel & Casino

5223 North Orient Road, Tampa; tel: 813-627-7625; www.seminolehardrocktampa.com; $$$

Owned and run by the Seminole tribe, this Hard Rock Hotel is a great place to stay in Tampa for those who enjoy gaming. The gleaming white tower with its 50ft (15-meter) Hard Rock guitar in front is visible from miles away. The 24-hour casino is chock full of memorabilia from rock 'n' roll legends; some items have touch-screens for background history and music videos. Rooms are large and chic. A beautiful pool with cabanas, several good restaurants, and a full-service spa and fitness center provide more places to play.

Chef Art Smith's Homecomin' Kitchen at Disney Springs

RESTAURANTS

Walt Disney World Resort

Chef Art Smith's Homecomin' Kitchen

Disney Springs, 1602 Buena Vista Drive; tel: 407-560-0100; www.homecominkitchen. com; daily lunch and dinner; $$

For a taste of the Deep South, dine at this rustic-feel restaurant, where celebrity chef Art Smith embraces his family's culinary heritage by serving up classics like buttermilk-brined fried chicken, shrimp 'n' grits, and hummingbird cake. For a quick bite, pick up a fried catfish sandwich with some moonshine from the grab-and-go window.

Chefs de France

Epcot World Showcase, France Pavilion; tel: 407-939-3463; daily lunch and dinner; $$

The more accessible of France's two table-service restaurants (although the other, the über-foodie Monsieur Paul, is spectacular), this bustling French brasserie feels just like a typical Parisian café and the food is true to its Champs-Élysée roots, from a lunchtime *salade niçoise* to a *steak-frites* dinner.

Flying Fish

Disney's BoardWalk Inn & Villas, 2101 Epcot Resorts Boulevard; tel: 407-939-3463; daily dinner; $$$

If you need a seafood fix, head to the festive boardwalk with free nightly entertainment, and duck into Flying Fish, a chef-driven restaurant with ambitious underwater-themed decor. This is fine dining with a fish and shellfish focus.

Frontera Cocina by Rick Bayless

Disney Springs, 1604 Buena Vista Drive; tel: 407-560-9197; www.fronteracocina. com; daily lunch and dinner, bar open late; $$

Chicago superchef Rick Bayless brings his signature Mexican specialties to Disney Springs, wowing with items from creative margaritas served in glasses rimmed with a spice-blend to deeply flavorful enchiladas. A take-out window serves tacos and margaritas to go; enjoy them at nearby alfresco seats.

Jiko – The Cooking Place

Disney's Animal Kingdom Lodge, 2901 Osceola Parkwa; tel: 407-939-3463; daily dinner; $$$

The flavors of Africa merge in exciting ways with American-friendly meats and veggies at this inventive hotel res-

Throughout this book, price guide for a two-course meal for one with an alcoholic drink:
$$$ = above US$50
$$ = US$25–50
$ = below US$25

Spice Road Table serves up tasty Moroccan fare

taurant, which boasts an astounding number of South African wines. For a less expensive foray into south-of-the-equator cuisine, dine across the hall at Boma, where similar spices make food vibrant in a tastefully designed smorgasbord format.

Planet Hollywood Observatory

Disney Springs, 1506 Buena Vista Drive; tel: 407-827-7827; http://planethollywood intl.com/restaurants/orlando/; daily lunch and dinner; $$

Newly redesigned in a grand way, the multi-floor flagship unit of this all-American hamburger chain features not only a sub-menu of sandwiches by celebrity chef Guy Fieri, but also a domed ceiling with a 4,500-sq-ft (418-sq-meter) immersive video wall. Wardrobe items from Hollywood films make the restaurant part museum, too. For example, the baseball uniform Madonna wore in *A League of Their Own* is displayed on the third floor.

The Polite Pig

Disney Springs, 1536 Buena Vista Drive; tel: 407-938-7444; www.politepig.com; daily lunch and dinner; $–$$

Smoked meats, Southern specialties, homemade brews and cocktails distinguish this counter-service barbecue restaurant at Disney Springs. There's a contemporary urban feel and warm brick touches. Craft beers, mixed drinks (try the tequila and grapefruit) and even wines are on tap. It's owned by one of Orlando's most respected restaurant groups, and the attention to quality is visible, from the scratch-made sauces to the doting service. Be sure to end your meal with a slice of moist Orange Blossom Honey Cake.

Spice Road Table

Epcot World Showcase, Morocco Pavilion; tel: 407-939-3463; daily lunch and dinner; $$

The exotic flavors of the Middle East beckon at this casual indoor-outdoor restaurant and bar, where small plates and entrées like coriander-crusted rack of lamb transport you to another continent. If time or budget don't allow for a Spice Road Table meal, get a flavorful, healthful fast-food fix at Morocco's Tangierine Café instead.

Universal Orlando Resort

Emeril's Restaurant Orlando

Universal CityWalk, 6000 Universal Boulevard; tel: 407-224-2424; www.emerils.com; daily lunch and dinner; $$$

This sophisticated restaurant features the creations of celebrity chef Emeril Lagasse. Assertive Creole flavors bubble up through artfully prepared specialties like grilled pork chop with caramelized sweet potatoes. Wine connoisseurs can choose from more than 10,000 bottles. The desserts are equally glorious as homey favorites like root beer float and banana cream pie become decadent masterpieces.

Indulgent milkshakes at the Toothsome Chocolate Emporium & Savory Feast Kitchen

Hard Rock Café Orlando

6050 Universal Boulevard; tel: 407-351-7625; www.hardrock.com; daily breakfast, lunch and dinner; $$

When it comes to theme restaurants, this is the big daddy of 'em all. The largest Hard Rock Café in the world, the walls here are plastered with gold records, album covers, flashy costumes, and instruments that have been strummed and drummed by some of the rock world's biggest names. Aretha Franklin's pink Cadillac revolves over the bar. The menu ranges from its legendary burgers to hickory smoked barbecue, but save room for the hot fudge brownie sundae. Free tours are available in the afternoons.

Mythos

Islands of Adventure, Lost Continent; tel: 407-224-3663; daily lunch and dinner; $$–$$$

The park's best restaurant is ensconced in a cavern with sculpted walls, purple upholstery, and lagoon views. Entrées include wood-roasted lobster with pad Thai, pan-roasted salmon with spicy tomato-fennel broth, and wood-fired flatbread – plus a very decent hamburger.

Toothsome Chocolate Emporium & Savory Feast Kitchen

Universal CityWalk, 6000 Universal Boulevard; tel: 407-224-3663; daily lunch and dinner; $$

Experience total immersion in the world of sweets at this bi-level restaurant, where a dipping counter, milkshake maker, chocolatier, and candy store will greet you – along with two costumed characters. Proceed to the dining room for a full menu of modern American fare – including chocolate-laced cocktails, but leave room for dessert, as that's what this highly themed restaurant is most about.

Downtown Orlando

Ace Cafe

100 W Livingston Street, Orlando; tel: 407-996-6686; www.acecafeusa.com; coffee bar daily from 7am, restaurant daily lunch and dinner; $

Three historic downtown Orlando buildings have been repurposed into the sprawling Ace Cafe, an offshoot of a 'motor diner'-themed London business of the same name. Within the complex are a coffee bar, full-service restaurant, bar, stage, retail shops, an art gallery, and motorcycle rentals. The Blue Cap Shack entertainment venue is under development.

East End Market

3201 Corrine Drive, Orlando; tel: 321-236-3316; www.eastendmkt.com; daily breakfast, lunch and (early) dinner; $–$$

Foodstuffs and meals of all sorts are on offer at this multi-vendor, local-oriented food hall, where Audubon Park Garden District residents meet neighbors over freshly squeezed juices and glasses of wine, and at the counters

Homemade pasta at The Rusty Spoon

selling breads, cookies, cheeses, and more. The communal outdoor seating areas are lovely. The ramen restaurant Domu has a moderately priced Japanese menu.

K Restaurant

1710 Edgewater Drive, Orlando; tel: 407-872-2332; www.krestaurant.net; daily dinner; $$

Home-grown superchef Kevin Fonzo serves up Italian and creative American fare in this freestanding College Park restaurant, where backyard garden wine parties with live music are part of the fun.

The Rusty Spoon

55 W Church Street, Orlando; tel: 407-499-8401; www.therustyspoon.com; daily dinner, Mon–Fri also lunch; $$

Chef-owner Kathleen Blake brings a California farm-to-table sensibility and Iowa wholesomeness to downtown Orlando, buying ingredients from local producers, making pastas from scratch, and taking every dish seriously, from the ultra-fresh salads to the stuffed burger and robust 'Dirty South' seafood stew. The craft cocktails are a bonus.

Reyes Mezcaleria

821 North Orange Ave, Orlando; tel: 407-373-0622; www.reyesmex.com; daily dinner, also Sun lunch; $

A bright, bustling dining room mixing earthy tones, urban flair and residential-style knick-knacks is the backdrop for chef-prepared regional Mexican specialities, both familiar and exotic.

Soco

629 E Central Boulevard, Orlando; tel: 407-849-1800; www.socothorntonpark.com; daily dinner, Sunday also brunch; $$–$$$

Chef Greg Richie puts New Age-spins on Southern classics at this ambitious Thornton Park restaurant, which is also known for its extensive bourbon menu and see-and-be-seen sidewalk seating area. The chicken-fried cauliflower is especially popular.

International Drive and Sand Lake Road

A Land Remembered

Rosen Shingle Creek, 9939 Universal Boulevard, Orlando; tel: 407-996-3663; www.landrememberedrestaurant.com; daily dinner; $$$

If you want to try authentic Florida 'Cracker' foods without a rustic airboat backdrop, head to this hotel steakhouse named after Patrick Smith's novel and decorated with atmospheric photographs and artifacts from Florida's past. It features serious steaks from Harris Ranch and well-prepared seafood, plus heritage specialties like gator stew.

Café Tu Tu Tango

8625 International Drive, Orlando; tel: 407-248-2222; www.cafetututango.com; daily lunch and dinner, Sat–Sun also brunch;

Trendy Dragonfly

$–$$

With bohemian decor designed to resemble an artist's garret in Barcelona, this laid-back small-plates restaurant offers up an impressive array of international tapas-style dishes to be shared. To add to the experience, local artists paint, sculpt, or perform live as you eat, and their art is for sale in the restaurant.

Dragonfly

Dellagio, 7972 Via Dellagio Way, Orlando; tel: 407-370-3359; www.dragonfly restaurants.com/orlando-florida; daily dinner; $$

The beautiful people gather at this high-style Japanese restaurant, where hot items from the robata grill, and creatively rolled raw items, offer a ying-yang of Asian experiences. Dragonfly has two further Florida locations.

Nile Ethiopian Cuisine

7048 International Drive, Orlando; tel: 407-354-0026; www.nile07.com; daily dinner; $$

This African restaurant may be in the heart of International Drive, but food-driven locals seek it out regularly, scooping up its exotically flavoured fare with authentic spongy bread. Try a combo for two on your first visit so you can sample a variety of dishes.

Pio Pio

5803 Precision Drive, Orlando; tel: 407-248-6424; http://mypiopio.com; daily lunch and dinner; $–$$

Colombian specialties – especially the phenomenal roast chicken – are the main draw here, although a few Peruvian dishes like ceviche round out the menu. Portions are large, prices are moderate, and quality is high. Add a dollop of garlicky white or spicy green sauce to just about everything you're served for an extra treat.

Sharks Underwater Grill

SeaWorld, 7007 SeaWorld Drive; tel: 407/351-3600 or 1-800-327-2424; daily lunch and dinner; $$–$$$

Set beside the enormous Sharks Encounter aquarium, this restaurant inside SeaWorld has one entire dining-room wall exposed to the tank, letting you sit in awe of the magnificent creatures swimming past. The food here, mostly seafood, is quite good considering the theme-park setting. Park admission required.

Slate

8323 W Sand Lake Road, Orlando; tel: 407-500-7528; www.slateorlando.com; daily dinner, also lunch Fri, brunch Sat–Sun; $$

Atlanta's Concentrics group brings high-style meals at modest prices to the restaurant tucked in next to Trade Joe's. The food tends toward trendy, with wood-fired-roasting ubiquitous. The pizzas and cocktails are especially good. On the rare chilly night, sit by the fireplace.

Urbain 40

Dellagio, 8000 Villa Dellagio Way, Orlando; tel: 407-872-2640; urbain40.com; daily lunch and dinner; $$–$$$

Have a flatbread with a glass of wine, a full-on French or American dinner, or a cocktail in the swanky 1940s-theme bar (often with live music) at this sprawling restaurant, where patio seats overlook a fountain. Plans are afoot to exand the menu to include brunch and late-night fare options.

The Whiskey

The Fountains, 7563 W Sand Lake Road, Orlando; tel: 407-930-6517; www.downatthewhiskey.com; daily lunch; $$

This cozy, pubby spot may play up its vast variety of brown spirits, but locals know to duck in for one of Orlando's best hamburgers, best ordered with sweet potato or truffled fries. They also serve small plates – great for sharing – and are serious about their craft cocktails too.

Kissimmee and Celebration

Bruno's Italian Restaurant

8556 W Highway 192, Kissimmee; tel: 407-397-7577; http://brunos192.com; daily lunch and dinner; $–$$

Bruno's is a friendly Italian restaurant, popular with locals and visitors alike. Decor is bright, colorful and inviting. There's a good selection of seafood pastas, veal, and chicken entrées alongside classic pizzas.

Cafe d'Antonio

691 Front Street, Celebration; tel: 407-566-2233; http://cafedantonios.com; daily lunch and dinner; $$

Light yet cozy, this Italian restaurant with a patio and lakefront views has a wide menu ranging from thin-crust pizzas to wood-fired meats, plus plenty of pasta dishes. The list of desserts is extensive.

Columbia Restaurant

649 Front Street, Celebration; tel: 407-566-1505; www.columbiarestaurant.com; daily lunch and dinner; $$–$$$

The Celebration branch of this century-old family-run restaurant overlooks the lake and serves Spanish-Cuban cuisine. A community favorite, the dining rooms are old-world style, the walls are covered in artworks and photographs, and it also has an outdoor café and tapas bar.

El Tenampa Mexican Restaurant

565 W Irlo Bronson Memorial Highway, Kissimmee; tel: 407-390-1959; daily lunch and dinner; $-$$

Authentic Mexican specialties like *chilaquiles* and *tamales*, plus more Americanized items such as fajitas, are served in this festive family-owned restaurant. Bright murals on the wall reflect the cheerful vibe.

Kenzie's Steak House

Mystic Dunes Golf Club, Old Lake Wilson Road, 1 mile south of Hwy 192; tel: 407-

Prato's veal sweetbread tortellini

397-1981; www.mystic-dunes-resort.com; daily lunch and dinner; $$–$$$

It's worth going off the beaten track to find this pleasant, casual restaurant, located in the midst of the Mystic Dunes Golf Resort overlooking the 18th green. Eat in the large dining room or outdoors on the patio terrace. Mains include a selection of pizzas, pastas, and exquisite fish and meat dishes; sandwiches and salads are available if you're in the mood for something lighter. The Aloha Tiki Bar & Grille (also on site) offers small bites and a comprehensive drinks menu.

Winter Park

Bulla Gastrobar

110 S Orlando Avenue, Winter Park; tel: 321-214-6120; http://bullagastrobar.com; daily lunch and dinner; $$

You'll feel like you're in Barcelona at this buzzy Spanish restaurant and tapas bar, where trendinistas share garlic shrimp and truffled potato chips topped with egg at the inside and outside bars, or dine more leisurely on full-on entrées from braised short ribs to tuna in an heirloom tomato vinaigrette. The impressive paella is cooked in a charcoal-burning oven.

Luma on Park

290 S Park Avenue, Winter Park; tel: 407-599-4111; www.lumaonpark.com; daily dinner; $$–$$$

This is perhaps the finest dining experience you'll find on the sophisti-

cated Park Avenue restaurant scene, with ultra-modern decor and creative dishes prepared in the open kitchen. Seafood features heavily on the menu, from scallops to barramundi, and there are steaks and chops, too. The wine list consists of boutique winemakers, mostly from California, and uniquely, half-glasses are available for those who would like to change wines for each course yet remain upright. For a quicker bite, get a burger or pizza in the dining room or lounge.

Prato

124 N Park Avenue, Winter Park; tel: 407-262-0050; www.prato-wp.com; daily dinner, also lunch Wed–Sun; $$–$$$

Orlando's very best pasta, all made from scratch, is at the heart of this rustic-chic progressive Italian restaurant, where the ever-changing cocktails, pizzas, appetizers, and entrées all get the same chef-focused attention. Start with the *campagna* salad (split it – it's huge and filling) and share an appetizer (the meatballs are divine), then get one of the day's pastas.

The Ravenous Pig

565 W Fairbanks Avenue, Winter Park; tel: 407-628-2333; www.theravenouspig. com; daily lunch and dinner; $$–$$$

Part elegant gastropub, part Cask & Larder brewery, this is inarguably Winter Park's most talked-about restaurant.

Eating al-fresco in Winter Park

Its chefs recreate the menu regularly, often incorporating Florida and Southern favorites into the mix. Start with the gruyere biscuits and end with the pig-tails donuts. For less fuss, cross the parking lot to sister eatery Swine & Sons ($), a take-out shop and deli with quaintly mismatched seating and the same scratch-food focus.

The Space Coast

Dixie Crossroads

1475 Garden Street, Titusville; tel: 321-268-5000; www.dixiecrossroads.com; daily dinner; $–$$$

Go to Dixie Crossroads at an off hour if you loathe feeling like a tourist, but go you must. This large seafood restaurant draws hordes for its fresh seafood, but is most famous for its preparation of rock shrimp, a local crustacean that, when prepared well (and it is here) resembles much pricier lobster. Decor is colorful and fun with no frills.

Shark Pit Bar & Grill

4001 N Atlantic Avenue, Cocoa Beach; tel: 321-868-8957; www.cocoabeachsurf.com; daily lunch and dinner, Sat–Sun also breakfast; $$

Inside the massive Cocoa Beach Surf Company store, this laid-back restaurant and lounge lets you dine beside a gigantic aquarium that is home to sharks and exotic fish. The menu is relaxed too, with a tasty range of salads, sandwiches, seafood and grilled meat entrées, and great pizzas baked in the brick oven.

Tampa Bay

Ella's American Folk Art Café

5119 N Nebraska Avenue, Tampa; tel: 813-234-1000; www.ellasfolkartcafe.com; daily dinner; $

Hipsters, foodies, and the budget conscious converge at this Seminole Heights favorite, where intriguing foods, live music, and the visual arts live side by side. Garlic-mashed potatoes find their way into chimichangas, Mexican dishes are served beside a European-style chicken roulade, and curries, pizzas, and burgers all have their place.

Sea Salt

Sundial, 183 2nd Avenue North, 2nd floor, St. Pete; tel: 727-873-7964; http://seasaltstpete.com; daily lunch and dinner; $$$

Matching salts to foods is part of the magic behind this spiffy St. Pete seafood restaurant, which has gained national attention for its dishes, which are prepared with extreme care. With the use of 130 different (and often colorful) salts from around the world, chef Fabrizio Aielli adds a Venetian touch to a changing menu where seafood is king. Produce is organic, sustainable and fresh – sourced from local farmers and day boat fishermen. The place's 22ft (6.7-meter) tall wine cellar contains 4,000 bottles of wine.

NIGHTLIFE

Nightlife in Orlando spans the category, even if you discount the nightly family-friendly firework shows accompanied by thundering music at many theme parks, and the themed dinner theater shows in the tourist corridors. Serious night owls gather at sizzling nightclubs, sophisticated cocktail bars, and casual beer-centered joints. Here's a sampling of the best after-hours spots in town.

Bars

The Courtesy

114 N Orange Avenue, Orlando; tel: 407-450-2041; www.thecourtesybar.com; Mon and Sat 7pm–2am, Tue–Fri 5pm–2am, Sun 3pm–2am

This star among Orlando's cocktail purveyors is so serious about mixology that its staff even teaches cocktail classes. Located Downtown.

Cowgirls Rockbar

I-Drive 360, 8371 International Drive, Suite 80, Orlando; tel: 407-930-3654; www.cowgirlsrockbar.com; Mon–Fri 4pm–2am, Sat–Sun 11am–2am

A mechanical bull and DJs make this I-Drive spot more bar than restaurant. The country-western theme creates an upbeat atmosphere.

Herman's Loan Office

22 W Pine Street, Orlando; tel: 407-649-0000; www.hermansloanoffice.com; Tue–Thu and Sat 8pm–2am, Fri 5pm–2am

Tiny and cozy, this quirky craft-cocktail bar creates drinks based on customer preferences, and offers punches to groups.

Hourglass Brewery

480 S Ronald Reagan Boulevard, Longwood, tel: 407-262-0056; http://thehourglassbrewery.com; Sun–Thu 11am–midnight, Fri–Sat until 2am

The beer is made on the premises at this 240-seat Longwood taproom, which embraces the owners' geekiness by providing game consoles. Live music and comedy are common.

The Imperial

1800 N Orange Avenue, Orlando; tel: 407-228-4992; www.imperialwinebar.com; Mon–Thu 5pm–midnight, Fri–Sat 5pm–1am, Sun 4–11pm

Furniture store by day, lounge at night, this relaxing nightstop in Orlando's Ivanhoe district is a winner for atmosphere alone. An interesting assortment of wines and beers adds to the charm.

The Pub

Pointe Orlando, 9101 International Drive, Suite 1003, Orlando; 407-352-2305; http://experiencethepub.com/orlando; daily 11am–2am

Dancing the night away at The Groove

Brits homesick for the pub can get a fix at this I-Drive institution, with familiar foods and beverages.

Red Light, Red Light

2810 Corrine Drive, Orlando; tel: 407-893-9832; http://redlightredlightbeerparlour.com; Sun–Wed 5pm–midnight, Thu–Sat until 2am

Loads of Orlando places make their own beers now, but local suds lovers have long been enamored with this Audubon Park district place. In addition to three-dozen draft beers, Red Light stocks 300 bottled varieties.

Music venues

House of Blues

Disney Springs, 1490 E Buena Vista Drive, Orlando; tel: 407-934-2583; www.houseofblues.com/orlando

This cozy concert venue within Disney Springs is also known for a weekly Gospel brunch on Sundays.

The Social

54 N Orange Avenue, Orlando; tel: 407-246-1419; www.thesocial.org

Locals frequent this small concert venue with an indie bent.

Tin Roof

I-Drive 360, 8371International Drive, Orlando; tel: 407-270-7926; www.tinrooforlando.com

It may look like a shack, but this I-Drive hangout, themed as a place for musicians to linger on their nights off,

has food, drinks, and concerts by local artists.

Nightclubs

The Beacham

46 N Orange Avenue, Orlando; tel: 407-246-1419; www.thebeacham.com

A 1921 cinema that has become a downtown Orlando nightlife fixture for its live performances and dancing throngs.

Blue Martini Lounge

9101 International Drive Suite 1182; tel: 407-447-2583; http://bluemartinilounge.com); Mon–Fri 4pm–2am, Sat–Sun 3pm–2am

This glitzy, upscale, I-Drive dance club and bar, which often has live music, attracts the area's young professionals.

Mango's Tropical Café

8126 International Drive, Orlando; tel: 407-603-3820; www.mangos.com

This Latin-themed restaurant, bar, and dance club on International Drive serves a variety of mojitos and daiquiris.

The Groove

Universal CityWalk, 6000 Universal Boulevard, Orlando; tel: 407-224-2165; daily 9pm–2am

Pumping sound and impressive special effects are on offer at this vibrant multi-level nightclub at Universal's CityWalk. Expect video screens on the walls, individually themed bars, and dancing till the early hours.

Downtown Orlando and Lake Eola lit up by night

A–Z

A

Age restrictions

You have to be over 21 to drink alcohol. Even if you are considerably older than that you should carry photo identification with you. If you cannot prove your age you will not be served.

Many of the rides in theme parks specify height restrictions. Check the relevant website for details.

B

Business hours

Outside the resorts most businesses are open from 9am or 10am to 5pm or later, with many of the shopping malls opening at 10am and remaining open as late as 10pm. Many large supermarkets, like Walmart, and a few restaurants, stay open 24 hours.

Banks usually remain open until at least 4pm from Monday to Thursday, and until 6pm on Friday. Some banks are open for a short time on Saturday.

During some public holidays local banks, businesses and stores may close.

C

Climate

Central Florida has a subtropical climate with high humidity. Summer daytime temperatures average 80°F–90°F (27°C–32°C) but can feel much hotter in July and August with humidity levels often in the high 90s. Winter weather is dry and temperate with daytime temperatures averaging 71°F–80°F (22°C–27°C), though they can drop surprisingly low at night.

Between May and September (especially June and July) heavy thunderstorms occur almost every afternoon but they are usually short in duration. Florida is unofficially dubbed the 'lightning capital of the country' because of the amount of strikes. The worst-hit area is west of Orlando by the Gulf Coast, but all of Central Florida receives its abundant share.

If you see a storm approaching, take cover. If you are in a car stay inside until the storm passes; many lightning victims are killed when getting into or out of their cars. If you are in a building do not 'make a run for it.' Do not use an umbrella during a lightning storm. Boaters should head for the nearest place they can tie up and evacuate the boat. During any nearby lightning storm parks will close their outdoor attractions.

Florida ranks eighth on the list of US states with the most tornadoes per year. However, they are not nearly as bad as the twisters that assail the Midwest. June to November is hurricane season in Florida. Orlando is more

Look out for alligators

protected from hurricanes than the coastal cities.

Clothing

Theme parks require a great deal of walking so be sure to bring comfortable shoes. If you plan on visiting a water park bring water shoes as well. Heavy rains occur daily in June and July so pack a rain poncho; umbrellas attract lightning and are therefore discouraged. Temperatures can get chilly in mid-winter so pack accordingly. Dress is casual in all but the highest-end restaurants.

Crime and safety

Although Orlando is not a high crime area it pays to take the same precautions you would take in any city. Watch your wallet or handbag in crowded places and never leave valuable items unattended. Keep money and jewelry in your hotel safe. Keep the hotel room and patio doors locked even when you are in the room. Don't open the door unless you know who is there; use the safety chain or check with the front desk if in doubt.

When driving keep doors locked and only park in well-lit areas. Never leave valuables in your car. If you have to, cover them up.

Theme parks conduct bag searches for all visitors and generally have good security.

Never approach or try to feed wildlife, especially alligators. Watch where you step when walking near a lake shore or a wetland area.

Customs regulations

There is no limit on the amount of money that you may bring in or take out of the US. However, you must declare amounts exceeding $10,000 or the foreign currency equivalent.

Customs allowances

Alcohol: Visitors over the age of 21 are permitted to bring in 34fl oz (1 liter) of alcohol for their personal use. Excess quantities are subject to duty and tax.

Cigars and cigarettes: Visitors may bring in no more than 200 cigarettes (one carton) or 100 cigars as part of their $800 duty exemption. An additional 100 cigars may be brought in under the gift exemption.

Gifts: As a visitor to the US you can claim on entry up to $100 worth of merchandise, free of duty and tax, as gifts for other people. Such articles may have to be inspected so do not gift-wrap them until after you have entered the country.

Prohibited goods

Articles that visitors are forbidden to take into the US include these: dangerous drugs, obscene publications, hazardous articles (e.g. fireworks) and narcotics.

Travelers using medicines containing narcotics (such as tranquilizers or cough medicine) should carry a prescription and/or a note from their doctor and should only take the quantity required for their stay. The medicine must be in its original container and clearly

Florida oranges

labelled. The medication must also be a legal prescription drug in the US.

Meat, poultry, fruit, vegetables, most dairy, absinthe, and more than 9 ounces (250 grams) of caviar are all prohibited.

D

Disabled travelers

Accessibility and facilities are excellent at the theme parks and other attractions in Orlando. Special parking is available near the entrances to each park, the hotels and other facilities. Visitors from outside the country can obtain a special parking permit by bringing a copy of their handicapped parking permit from home, photo ID (passport) and $15 to a Florida vehicle licensing bureau. Visit www.flhsmv.gov to find a location.

Wheelchairs are available to rent from several locations, usually near the park's entrance. For some rides guests may remain in wheelchairs but for others they must be able to leave them. Regulations are indicated in leaflets and at the appropriate entrance. Nearly all buses can accommodate conventional wheelchairs and access is available at toilets in all the theme parks.

Guests with disabilities should request, or get online, Disney World's 'Guide for Guests with Disabilities,' which spells out offerings for those with mobility, visual and hearing issues. Also online and at each park's Guest Services window are park-specific guides. Offerings for the hearing impaired, for example, include handheld, reflective and video captioning in certain places. A sign-language interpreter is available for certain theater shows on rotating days. Those with vision impairment might want to use a handheld device with audio descriptions or Braille guidebooks and maps.

Universal Orlando, SeaWorld and Legoland all have downloadable guides with information for people with disabilities on their websites.

E

Electricity

You will need an adapter for British and European plugs, as well as a voltage transformer. US sockets take flat two-pronged plugs, sometimes with a third round prong. The power supply is 110–120 volts AC (60 cycles).

Embassies and consulates

Most embassies are in Washington DC. These are the nearest consulates for English-speaking countries:

Australia: (Honorary Consul, by appointment only) Law Offices of Slesnick and Casey, LLP, 2701 Ponce de Leon Boulevard, Suite 20, Coral Gables, FL 33134; tel: 786-505-6802.

Canada: 200 South Biscayne Boulevard, Suite 1600, Miami, FL 33131; tel: 305-579-1600.

New Zealand: 37 Observatory Circle, NW, Washington DC 20008; tel: 202-328-4800.

Playing mini-golf at Universal Citywalk

Republic of Ireland: (Honorary Consul, by appointment only) Law Offices of Terence J Delahunty, Jr P.A, 118 East Jefferson Street, Suite 203, Orlando, FL 32801; tel: 401-810-3352.

South Africa: 333 East 38th Street, 9th Floor, New York, NY 10016; tel: 212-213-4880.

UK: 1001 Brickell Bay Dr., Miami, FL 33131; tel: 305-400-6400.

Emergency numbers

For police, ambulance or fire services dial: 911.

Gay and lesbian travelers

For a few days every June, Orlando and its theme parks host Gay Days. Thousands of gay and lesbian travelers come to join in the special gay-oriented celebrations. For more details, visit www.gaydays.com.

Golf

Orlando has more than 150 golf courses and more than 20 golf academies, including many signature courses designed by famous golf pros. Orlando also hosts many professional golf tournaments. Visitor options range from public courses, where you can play a casual round, to all-inclusive golf resorts. For information on the range of golf resorts and facilities visit www.visitorlandogolf.com or www.golfersguide.com/orlando.

H

Health

If you need medical assistance speak to the reception staff at your hotel. The larger resort hotels may have a resident doctor; if not, the staff can help you find the nearest doctor or hospital. The Orlando area has several 'urgent care' walk-in clinics, where visitors need no appointment and those without insurance pay a set price for each service. CentraCare (https://centracare.org/florida), affiliated with the Florida Hospital chain, is one that has several outlets. For small medical issues many CVS (www.cvs.com/minuteclinic) and Walgreens (www.walgreens.com/topic/pharmacy/healthcare-clinic.jsp) pharmacies have clinics.

Insurance: The cost of any health care is exorbitant. Never leave home without adequate travel insurance; a minimum cover of $1 million unlimited medical cover is strongly recommended. Carry an identification card or policy number at all times to ensure you receive prompt treatment.

Pharmacies: Always bring enough prescription medicine from home to cover the length of your trip.

For over-the-counter medicines go to Walgreens or CVS; many are open 24 hours. Walmart, Target, Publix and other grocery retailers also have pharmacy sections.

Health hazards: The two most common health hazards in Orlando are sunburn and heat exhaustion; both are easily

Fantastical Cinderella Castle

avoided. Use a high-factor sun cream and wear a hat and sunglasses.

The heat alone can be a danger, especially for the elderly or those with a pre-existing medical condition. Dehydration and salt deficiency can lead to heat exhaustion. The main symptoms are headache, weakness, light-headedness, muscle aches, cramps, and agitation. Make a point of drinking plenty of non-alcoholic fluids (before you get thirsty) and take periodic breaks in the shade or in an air-conditioned environment.

If untreated, heat exhaustion can escalate to a far more serious case of heatstroke, which means that the body's temperature rises to dangerous levels. In addition to the symptoms listed above people suffering from heatstroke may exhibit confusion, strange behavior and even seizures. If you suspect a companion is suffering from heatstroke get that person to a cool place, apply cold damp cloths and call 911 immediately.

I

Internet

There is free wireless internet access at Orlando International Airport, most hotels (in the room or public areas), many of the theme parks and coffee bars.

L

Lost property

If you lose an item at one of the theme parks check with Guest Services who will direct you to the park's lost property office.

M

Maps

Florida tourist offices (including overseas) often distribute the Florida Official Transportation Map (www.visitflorida. com), which has city plans, free of charge. Would-be visitors can order the map in advance. You will also find a variety of free general maps showing main sections of the Orlando area at hotels and tourist centers. The Insight Flexi map of Orlando is laminated and very practical.

Media

Newspapers: The *Orlando Sentinel* is the city's daily newspaper. *Orlando Weekly*, published on Thursdays, is the region's alternative paper for news, opinion, arts and entertainment. The national daily, *USA Today*, is distributed free at many hotels.

Magazines: The monthly *Orlando Magazine* has interesting feature articles on the arts, entertainment, dining and general lifestyle. A good source for monthly listings and information is *WhereTraveler* magazine, distributed free at many hotels.

Radio: Highlights of Orlando's many stations include WMFE 90.7 (public radio for news and information), WBDO 96.5 (news), WMMO 98.9 (classic rock), The Wolf 103.1 (country), WDBO 580 (sports) and WUCF 89.9 (jazz).

Television: Among the dozens of chan-

nels, usually accessed via cable or satellite, are Central Florida News 13 (only accessible via Spectrum cable's Channel 13), WMFE-TV-PBS, WFTV-ABC, WKMG-CBS and WESH-NBC. Channel numbers depend on the access system.

Money

Currency: The currency in the US is the dollar, divided into 100 cents. Coins come in denominations of 1 cent (penny), 5 cents (nickel), 10 cents (dime) and 25 cents (quarter). There are a limited number of 50-cent (half-dollar) and dollar coins in circulation. Dollar bills (notes) come in $1, $5, $10, $20, $50, $100 and $500.

Travelers' Checks: Nearly every tourist-oriented business in Orlando accepts credit cards. Foreign visitors who prefer to use cash are advised to take US dollar travelers' checks to Orlando. Changing foreign currency, whether as cash or checks, can prove problematic. You can seek out currency exchange facilities at busy centers like retail malls, but generally they are hard to find.

Cash Machines: You can take money out at ATM (automatic teller machine) with a debit or credit card using your PIN. Cash machines are widespread around the city. The most widely accepted cards are Visa, American Express, Mastercard, Diners Club and Discover. Maestro cards are often not accepted.

Be sure to check the rate of exchange and any other charges your financial institution may levy before using your card abroad. Some charge prohibitive rates. ATM operators usually apply a charge but you will be notified of this on-screen before you complete the transaction.

Credit Cards: Credit cards are very much part of daily life in Orlando and can be used to pay for almost everything. Car rental firms and hotels will usually take an imprint of your card as a deposit.

Post

Post offices: The opening hours of post offices vary between central, big-city branches and those in smaller towns, but all are open Monday–Friday (generally 8 or 9am–5pm) and some open on Saturday mornings. Supermarkets (at the customer service counter), pharmacies and hotels usually have a small selection of stamps, and there are stamp-vending machines in some transport terminals. You can also print postage online at www.usps.com.

Delivery services: For the best service choose Priority Mail Express via the US postal service. It guarantees next-day delivery within the US and delivery within two to three days to foreign destinations. Privately owned courier services, which offer next-day delivery to most places can be accessed online. Contact info for the main services are as follows:

US Postal Service: 800-275-8777, www.usps.com

FedEx: 800-463-3339, www.fedex.com/us

DHL: 800-225-5435, www.dhl-usa.com

UPS: 800-742-5877, www.ups.com

Mickey's Once Upon a Christmastime Parade

Public holidays

Jan 1 New Year's Day
Jan (third Mon) Martin Luther King Day
Feb (third Mon) Presidents' Day
Mar/Apr Good Friday (optional)
May (last Mon) Memorial Day
July 4 Independence Day
Sept (first Mon) Labor Day
Oct (second Mon) Columbus Day
Nov 11 Veterans' Day
Nov (last Thu) Thanksgiving
Dec 25 Christmas Day

R

Religion

Nearly every faith and denomination is represented in Orlando. To find an appropriate place of worship, type in the denomination online and use Google Maps to find the closest matches.

S

Smoking

Smoking is not permitted in restaurants, most public buildings and areas, or at theme parks, although they all have designated smoking areas. Hotels are predominantly non-smoking, although many have smoking rooms; specify your preference when booking.

Taxes

A Florida sales tax of 6 percent is added to all merchandise at the sales counter except for necessary medicine and grocery items. Orange County, home to Orlando and Disney World, adds on 0.5 percent for a total sales tax of 6.5 percent. In addition, a Tourist Development tax of up to 6 percent is levied on hotel rooms. Both taxes vary by county.

Telephones

Phone numbers: US telephone numbers have a 3-digit area code followed by a 7-digit number. Area codes for the Orlando metro region are 407 and 321. You should dial all 10 digits when making a call. To call a number outside this area code you should first dial '1'. These calls will incur long-distance charges unless you have a national mobile-phone plan. Toll-free numbers generally have the prefix 800, 888 or 866; you may need to dial a '1' when calling these numbers. Cell phone (mobile) numbers have 10 digits, the same as regular phone numbers.

Calling from abroad: To call Orlando from the UK dial 00 (international code) + 1 (USA) + the area code and number. To call other countries from the USA first dial the international code (011) then the country code: Australia 61, Germany 49, Ireland 353, New Zealand 64 and UK 44, followed by the number. Dial Canadian numbers as you would a long-distance US number.

Public telephones: Phone booths are hard to find in public areas. You are better off buying a disposable mobile phone at a retailer like Walmart or buying cards

Playing arcade games at WonderWorks

with prepaid minutes from convenience stores, service stations and other outlets.

Time zones

Orlando is on Eastern Standard Time (EST). It is 5 hours behind Greenwich Mean Time (GMT) and 3 hours ahead of Pacific Standard Time. It observes Daylight Saving Time (1 hour ahead) from mid-March through October.

Tipping

Service personnel expect tips in Orlando. The accepted rate for baggage handlers in airports is $5 per bag. For others, including taxi drivers and waiters, 15–20 percent is the going rate. Sometimes tips are included in restaurant bills so be sure to check carefully before adding on gratuity.

Moderate hotel tipping is around $2 per bag or suitcase handled by porters or bellboys. It is not necessary to tip chamber staff unless you stay several days. $3–5 per day is usual, depending on the state of your room and length of stay, more in high-end hotels.

Tour operators

It's easier than ever to get around Orlando using the free Visit Orlando destination app (www.visitorlando.com/plan-your-trip/visit-orlando-destination-app), but plenty of operators will guide you around town for a day or a week, or for a select activity like a fishing excursion.

Gray Line Orlando, using the local name **Gator Tours**, is one such sightseeing company. It offers a city tour of Orlando, half-day and full-day tours of the local area, tours to attractions, deep-sea fishing trips and other activities; www.gatortours.com; tel: 407-522-5911.

Orlando Tours offers a huge variety of coach tours and activity tours, including airboat rides, animal and wildlife tours, boat tours, cruises, visits to all the major attractions and bus trips to other Florida cities; www.orlando-tours.com; tel: 1-800-303-5107.

American Ghost Adventures has a two-hour walking tour of haunted sites in downtown Orlando, including a chance to conduct your own paranormal investigation using specialized equipment; http://americanghostadventures.com; tel: 407-256-6225.

Orlando Food Tours is one of a few local outfits bringing food-curious travelers to several tastings in one excursion. They are walking tours around a single food-worthy neighbourhood; www.orlandofoodtours.com; tel: 800-656-0713.

Tourist information

In Orlando: The Official Visitor Center is at 8723 International Drive, Suite 101, Orlando, FL 32819; tel: 407-363-5872; www.visitorlando.com. It is located at the corner of I-Drive and Austrian Row and is open daily from 8.30am to 6.30pm. This is a good one-stop source for information about the area where you can also pick up free maps, brochures, buy discounted theme-park and attractions tickets and book hotels. Satellite offices are located at The Mall at Millenia Concierge Desk

The view over the Orlando Eye and I–Drive

and inside the Fort Drum and West Palm Florida's Turnpike rest stops. You can live-chat with a specialist online 9am–5pm weekdays (www.visitorlando.com/plan-your-trip/visitor-center) and buy tickets on the site at your leisure. Do not purchase tickets from an unauthorized vendor; the tickets may not work and you will have wasted your money.

In the UK: For a free holiday-planning kit, visit www.visitorlando.com/vacation-planning-kit. Get the Disney World version at tel: 0800-169-0730; or visit www.disneyholidays.co.uk/walt-disney-world/free-planning-tools. Universal's can be found at www.universalorlandoresort.com/uk/dvd_order.html; SeaWorld Orlando's is at www.seaworldparks.co.uk/order-a-free-dvd.

Transportation

Arrival

By car: From the north, interstate highways I-95, I-75 and I-10 bring you into Florida. They connect with I-4, US 192, Highway 528 and the Florida Turnpike which run through the Orlando metro area. From the south, Orlando is reached via I-75, I-95 and the Florida Turnpike.

By bus: Greyhound (tel: 800-231-2222; from outside the US 214-849-8100; www.greyhound.com) provides bus services to Florida and all over the state.

By rail: Amtrak (tel: 800-872-7245; www.amtrak.com) offers slow and leisurely services from America's Midwest, northeast and south and connecting services from points west to certain Florida

cities. For those who want to take their car along they also offer an Auto Train service from Lorton Virginia to Sanford.

By air: Most major US and international carriers serve Orlando. Fare prices are competitive. Scheduled services are supplemented by charter flights, most of which fly into Orlando Sanford International Airport, about 45 minutes north of the city.

Airports

Orlando International Airport (www.orlandoairports.net): International airlines fly direct or via other US cities into Orlando International Airport, 9 miles (14km) south of downtown Orlando and about 25 miles (40km) from Walt Disney World Resort. It has two terminals (with a third on the way). Tel: 407-825-2001 (general inquiries), 407-825-8463 (flight information).

Local buses depart from the A side of the Main Terminal on Level 1. Lynx buses 11, 42, 51, 111, 407 and 436S serve the airport. Travel time to downtown Orlando is approximately 40 minutes. Lynx bus 42 serves International Drive; travel time is around 60 minutes. Fares are $2.

Taxis are located on both the A and B sides of the Main Terminal at the Ground Transportation Level (level 1). Metered rates vary, but fares range from $35 to Downtown, $38 to International Drive, $60 to Kissimmee, and $69 to Walt Disney World.

Shuttle vans also operate from this location; fares per person range from

Different modes of transport on Main Street USA

$11–44, depending on the destination.

All the major car rental firms have facilities at the airport.

Orlando Sanford Airport (www.orlandosanfordairport.com): Most vacation charter flights arrive at Sanford Airport, about 30 miles (48km) north of Orlando. Though it's conveniently located off I-4, the extra distance can be costly if you plan to use a taxi or shuttle bus to reach Orlando. The major car rental firms are represented at the airport. Tel: 407-585-4000.

Transport within Orlando

Bus: The Orlando metro area has an excellent public bus system, called Lynx. It serves most of the popular theme parks, attractions and shopping malls, as well as the airports. Bus stops are marked in pink with the paw print of a lynx cat or a bus.

A single fare is $2. An all-day pass costs $4.50. You can buy both from the bus driver but exact change is required. Seven-day and 30-day passes for unlimited rides are also available from the visitor center (see page 129).

Lynx usually runs every day, though some schedules change, and buses may not run on Sundays and holidays. Schedules are available at the visitor center or online at www.golynx.com. For more information, contact customer service on 407-841-5969.

The Lymmo bus system in downtown Orlando provides free transportation around Downtown. Four routes are currently in operation: Link 60 (Orange– Downtown Line), Link 61 (Lime Line), Link 62 (Grapefruit Line) and Link 63 (Orange–North Quarter Line). Lymmo buses run on their own lanes and control their own stoplights, ensuring they are not slowed down by other traffic.

I-Ride trolley: These trolleys run to all the attractions, hotels and shopping malls along International Drive from the outlet malls south of SeaWorld up to the northernmost outlet mall. They operate daily 8am–10.30pm. Single fares are $2 and exact change is required. Children aged three to nine ride for $1. You can also buy passes for unlimited rides for three, five, seven, or 14 days (you must buy them in advance from one of the outlets listed on www.iridetrolley.com/passes.asp); they cost from $7 to $18. For more information, tel: 407-354- 5656; www.iridetrolley.com.

Taxis: Cabs are plentiful throughout the Orlando area, but they are not cheap and you need to phone in advance for pick-up. Your hotel can do this for you. Alternatively, several companies are listed in phone and online directories. Visitors with internet access often find smartphone app services like Uber (www.uber.com) and Lyft (www.lyft.com) to be easier to use and less expensive. Downtown, bicycle-driven pedicabs are a fun and inexpensive way to get around.

Car rental: Renting a car is the easiest way to explore Orlando. However, you may encounter some traffic on the major roads. If possible, avoid driving the I-4 corridor during rush hour (7–10am and 4–7pm).

Go-karting at Fun Spot

Most rental agencies require you to be 21 years old (sometimes 25), have a valid driver's license and a major credit card to rent a vehicle. Foreign travelers can use the licence issued in their home country.

Visitors wishing to rent a car upon arrival in Orlando will find rental offices at the airports, downtown locations and even at some hotels. Rates are cheap by US and international standards. Local rental firms outside the airports are often less expensive than the national companies. Insurance is usually optional, but non-US residents should buy it since their regular insurance might not be sufficient.

It is normally cheaper to arrange car rental in advance. You should check with your airline or travel agent for special package deals that include a car. However, be wary of offers of 'free' car rental, which do not include extras like tax and insurance.

Be sure to check that your car-rental agreement includes a Loss Damage Waiver (LDW), also known as Collision Damage Waiver (CDW). Without it, you will be liable for any damage done to your vehicle in the event of an accident, regardless as to whether or not you were to blame. You are advised to pay for supplementary Liability Insurance on top of the standard third-party insurance. US drivers can normally use their personal car insurance to cover a rental vehicle.

Many Orlando roads have tolls, and many car rental agencies offer the use of an electronic toll-paying device called Sunpass or Epass, giving you unlimited access to the drive-through lanes. The toll roads are pricy, but generally much quicker than parallel roads.

Driving

Getting around Orlando by car is generally easy, though traffic is heavy on some routes. Road signs are good and exits for major attractions and areas are well marked. Use a current map as roads change, with new ones being added regularly in Central Florida. Built-in car GPSs are generally out of date.

Traffic conditions: I-4 can become heavily congested, especially during rush hour. Plus, it is in the early stages of a massive 10-year expansion and renovation, so traffic is always unpredictable. For current traffic conditions dial 511 (or check online at www.FL511.com); this is the Florida Department of Transportation's free hotline for up-to-date traffic information, construction and severe weather reports on all Florida interstate highways (including I-4).

Rules of the road: Driving is on the right. You must carry your driving license at all times or you can be fined. Unless there is a sign prohibiting it, you can turn right on a red light after making a complete stop and checking that the way is clear. Cars must stop for a school bus with its lights flashing and remain stopped until the bus drives off (this does not apply to a divided highway).

Seatbelts: These must be worn at all times by all passengers. Children aged five and under must be placed in

A dappled back road near St Petersburg

an approved child-safety seat. These should be available for a fee from car rental agencies.

Alcohol: Florida has some of the toughest laws in the US against driving under the influence, resulting in jail time, automatic loss of your license and stiff fines. The maximum level permitted is so small that you are advised to drink no alcohol at all if driving. It is also illegal to have an open container of alcohol in your vehicle.

Speed limits: American states set their own speed limits. In Florida they are: 55–70mph (85–110kph) on highways, 20–30mph (30–45kph) in residential areas and 15mph (20kph) near schools. Limits change suddenly and for only short distances so pay attention to signs. The Highway Patrol is good at enforcing limits, including minimum speed limits: signs along interstates sometimes oblige motorists to drive at over 40mph (65kph).

Gas (petrol): Fuel is sold in American gallons and comes in three grades of unleaded gasoline. Prices vary considerably. Many stations are open 24 hours.

Parking: Theme parks charge hefty parking fees (up to $20 for a car). Parking is free at shopping malls, most museums and other attractions. In large lots, take a picture of the lot name and row number so you can find your car after sightseeing. Street parking is limited in downtown Orlando; it is best to use parking garages. Look for signs indicating parking restrictions and tow-away zones. Park in the same direction as the flow of traffic and do not park on the curb.

Visas and passports

Most foreign visitors need a machine-readable passport (which should be valid for at least six months longer than their intended stay) and a visa to enter the US. You should also be able to prove your intention to leave the US after your visit (usually a return or onward ticket). Visitors from some countries need an international vaccination certificate.

Certain foreign nationals are exempt from the normal visa requirements. Canadian citizens with a valid Canadian passport do not need a visa.

Under the 'visa-waiver' program, citizens of 38 countries do not require a visa if they are staying for less than 90 days and have a round-trip or onward ticket. These include the UK, Ireland, Australia, New Zealand, Japan, France and Germany. If you travel under this program, you'll still need to obtain an Electronic System for Travel Authorization (ESTA) before arrival, which can be found online for a small fee.

Those requiring a visa or information can apply by mail or personal application to their local US Embassy or Consulate.

W

Weights and measures

The imperial system is used in the US. Metric weights and measures are rarely used.

Adam Sandler in The Waterboy

BOOKS AND FILM

Jack Kerouac, famed author of *On the Road*, lived in a bungalow in Orlando's College Park neighborhood in the 1950s – which is where he wrote his classic novel, *The Dharma Bums*. However, Orlando isn't all about serious beatnik-esque writers suffering for their art (even though the market gets its fair play in books and on screen).

The theme-park community contributes greatly, as many animated films were illustrated at Disney World until the local animation studios closed in 2004. What's more, writers, actors, and producers staff these entertainment behemoths and, after hours, often seek additional outlets for their art.

Orlando sets the backdrop for many books and movies. Here is a sampling.

Books

Fiction
A Land Remembered, by Patrick D. Smith. This compelling tale of a pioneer family takes place, in large part, in Osceola County just south of Walt Disney World. Kissimmee, on its northern tip, is now home to many tourist attractions.

Down and Out in the Magic Kingdom, by Corey Doctorow. This fun-loving sci-fi novel has fun with the most iconic of Orlando's theme parks.

Fresh Off the Boat: A Memoir, by Eddie Huang. New York chef Eddie Huang's memoir about life as a Taiwanese-American in the United States. He lived in Orlando for part of his childhood. The memoir has since been made into TV series.

Paper Towns, by John Green. This young adult mystery, by the author of *The Fault in our Stars* (now a feature film) is set in Orlando.

Tangerine, by Edward Bloor. In this young adult novel a bespectacled boy and his family relocate to Central Florida.

Their Eyes Were Watching God, by Zora Neale Hurston. This timeless novel, a true American classic, was written in 1937. Strong and independent Janie Crawford returns to Etonville, north of Orlando, and recounts her captivating life tale.

Non-fiction
Cross Creek, by Marjorie Kinnan Rowlings. In this beautiful memoir, a city dweller trades in her urban life for one in the country north of Orlando.

Lost Orlando (Images of America), by Stephanie Gaub Antequino and Tana Mosier Porter, on behalf of the Historical Society of Central Florida. Orlando was a rough-and-ready Southern town for the most part, before Mickey Mouse moved in. This photo-heavy book shares architecture of decades gone by.

The Queen Of Versailles

Love Is Love, edited by Marc Andreyko. Comics by various artists in tribute to survivors of the 2016 Pulse nightclub shooting.

Mommy's Little Girl: Casey Anthony and her Daughter Caylee's Tragic Fate, by Diane Fanning. One of many books related to the sensational case of Orlando mother Casey Anthony, who was accused and acquitted of killing her young daughter.

Orlando, Florida: A Brief History, by James Clark. Historian, educator and journalist, James Clark takes readers back to Orlando's earliest days when the Seminoles lived here, then the cowboys, then the citrus farmers.

Project Future: The Inside Story Behind the Creation of Disney World, by Chad Denver Emerson. A behind-the-scenes look at how Walt Disney transformed Florida's wetlands into a theme-park empire.

Universal Orlando: The Unofficial Story, by Nick Sim. Real-life information about how the Universal Orlando complex came to be, by the man behind the www.themeparktourist. com blog.

Film

Apollo 13, 1995. Gripping retelling of the almost ill-fated Apollo 13 moon-landing mission, starring Tom Hanks.

Contact, 1996. This intense film is one of many space-related movies to have scenes shot on the Space Coast, starring Jodie Foster.

Ernest Saves Christmas, 1998. Holiday chuckles abound as a man claiming to be Santa Claus arrives in Orlando.

Escape from Tomorrow, 2013. Filmmaker Randy Moore shot many scenes at Disney World and Disneyland without permission to create this fantasy-horror about a man who is fired from his job on the last day of his theme-park family vacation.

Jaws 3-D, 1983. The third *Jaws* film, directed by Joe Alves, follows the Brody children as tragedy strikes SeaWorld Orlando. Two great whites infiltrate the park's underwater tunnels.

The Queen of Versailles, 2012. This entertaining documentary is about timeshare mogul David Siegel and his wife, Jacqueline, who are building an enormous Orlando-area house.

Sisters, 2015. A ridiculous American comedy starring popular comics Tina Fey and Amy Poehler, who have one last hurrah at their childhood Orlando home.

Sydney White 2007. A teen comedy filmed in the Orlando area, including at Rollins College in Winter Park and the University of Central Florida, starring Amanda Bynes.

The Waterboy, 1998. Many scenes from this sports comedy were filmed in Central Florida, including Camping World Stadium (then the Citrus Bowl), Stetson University in Deland and a cabin in Clermont. Starring Adam Sandler.

ABOUT THIS BOOK

This *Explore Guide* has been produced by the editors of Insight Guides, whose books have set the standard for visual travel guides since 1970. With top-quality photography and authoritative recommendations, these guidebooks bring you the very best routes and itineraries in the world's most exciting destinations.

BEST ROUTES

The routes in the book provide something to suit all budgets, tastes and trip lengths. As well as covering the destination's many classic attractions, the itineraries track lesser-known sights, and there are also excursions for those who want to extend their visit outside the city. The routes embrace a range of interests, so whether you are an art fan, a gourmet, a history buff or have kids to entertain, you will find an option to suit.

We recommend reading the whole of a route before setting out. This should help you to familiarise yourself with it and enable you to plan where to stop for refreshments – options are shown in the 'Food and Drink' box at the end of each tour.

For our pick of the tours by theme, consult Recommended Routes for… (see pages 6–7).

INTRODUCTION

The routes are set in context by this introductory section, giving an overview of the destination to set the scene, plus background information on food and drink, shopping and more, while a succinct history timeline highlights the key events over the centuries.

DIRECTORY

Also supporting the routes is a Directory chapter, with a clearly organised A–Z of practical information, our pick of where to stay while you are there and select restaurant listings; these eateries complement the more low-key cafés and restaurants that feature within the routes and are intended to offer a wider choice for evening dining. Also included here are some nightlife listings and our recommendations for books and films about the destination.

ABOUT THE AUTHORS

Rona Gindin is an Orlando-based travel writer whose adventures have taken her around the globe. She is the author of *The Little Black Book of Walt Disney World* (2013) and has contributed to several other books on Orlando. Gindin is an Orlando restaurant expert and shares her culinary escapades along with her travel discoveries on her website, www.ronagindin.com.

This book builds on content written by Donna Dailey.

CONTACT THE EDITORS

We hope you find this Explore Guide useful, interesting and a pleasure to read. If you have any questions or feedback on the text, pictures or maps, please do let us know. If you have noticed any errors or outdated facts, or have suggestions for places to include on the routes, we would be delighted to hear from you. Please drop us an email at hello@insightguides.com. Thanks!

CREDITS

Explore Orlando
Editor: Helen Fanthorpe
Authors: Rona Gindin and Donna Dailey
Head of Production: Rebeka Davies
Update Production: Apa Digital
Picture Editor: Tom Smyth
Cartography: original cartography Apa Cartography Department, updated by Carte
Photo credits: Alamy 4/5T, 35, 41, 46/47, 78, 79, 85L, 89L, 95, 134; Bill Serne/Visit Florida 98; Busch Gardens 96, 97L, 96/97; Chip Litherland/LEGOLAND Florida Resort 4ML, 6ML, 24ML, 102MC; Columbia Restaurant Group 117; Delaware North 12/13, 90, 92, 92/93; Dragonfly 116; Evergreen Pictures/REX/Shutterstock 135; Four Seasons 102/103T; Gareth Kelly/Visit Florida 101L; Getty Images 8/9T, 16/17, 22, 24/25T, 28/29, 34, 42/43, 81M, 93L, 94, 100/101; Goa Min/Visit Florida 8MC, 36T, 126; iStock 7M, 63, 76/77, 88/89, 122, 123; Jason Collier/SeaWorld 15, 59, 60; Julie Fletcher/Visit Florida 4MC, 6MC, 12, 24MC, 64, 66/67T, 68, 68/69, 70, 70/71, 82, 84, 86, 88, 115, 119, 120; Lara Cerri/Visit Florida 102MR; LEGOLAND Resort Florida 81T, 80/81T, 110; Leonardo 109, 111; Michael DeFreitas/roberthard/REX/Shutterstock 83; Nasa 90/91; Nowitz Photography/Apa Publications 6BC, 99, 100; Scott Audette/VisitFlorida 20, 102ML, 125; Scott Keeler/Visit Florida 19, 66, 67T; SeaWorld 24MR, 58, 61L, 60/61, 62; Shutterstock 10/11, 24MR, 64/65, 67M, 91L; Song Guanhua/Visit Florida 4MR, 20/21, 72, 130; SuperStock 73, 80, 87L, 86/87; The Kessler Collection 65L; Universal Orlando Resort 7MR, 8ML, 8ML, 8MR, 24ML, 50, 51, 52, 53L, 52/53, 54, 55L, 54/55, 56, 57L, 56/57, 102ML, 102MC, 102MR, 107, 108, 114, 121, 127; Visit Florida 4ML, 13L, 16, 18, 118, 124, 131, 133; Walt Disney World Resort 1, 4MC, 4MR, 6TL, 7T, 7MR, 8MC, 8MR, 14, 17L, 21L, 23, 24MC, 26, 27, 28, 29L, 30, 31, 32, 33L, 32/33, 36B, 37, 38B, 38T, 39L, 38/39, 40, 42, 43L, 44, 45, 46, 47L, 48B, 48T, 49L, 48/49, 104, 105, 106, 112, 113, 128; Willie J. Allen Jr/Visit Florida 71L, 74, 75L, 74/75, 84/85, 129, 132
Cover credits: iStock (main&bottom)

Printed by CTPS – China

First Edition 2017

DISTRIBUTION

UK, Ireland and Europe
Apa Publications (UK) Ltd
sales@insightguides.com
United States and Canada
Ingram Publisher Services
ips@ingramcontent.com
Australia and New Zealand
Woodslane
info@woodslane.com.au
Southeast Asia
Apa Publications (Singapore) Pte
singaporeoffice@insightguides.com
Hong Kong, Taiwan and China
Apa Publications (HK) Ltd
hongkongoffice@insightguides.com
Worldwide
Apa Publications (UK) Ltd
sales@insightguides.com

SPECIAL SALES, CONTENT LICENSING AND COPUBLISHING

Insight Guides can be purchased in bulk quantities at discounted prices. We can create special editions, personalised jackets and corporate imprints tailored to your needs.
sales@insightguides.com
www.insightguides.biz

INDEX

MAP LEGEND

●	Start of tour	✈	Airport		Important building
→	Tour & route direction	▭	Railway		Park
❶	Recommended sight	🚌	Main bus station		Urban area
❷	Recommended restaurant/café	𝗠	Museum/gallery		Hotels
★	Place of interest	🎭	Theatre		Shop / market
❶	Tourist information	➕	Church		Transport hub
		✉	Main post office		Non-urban area

INSIGHT ⊙ GUIDES
OFF THE SHELF

Since 1970, **INSIGHT GUIDES** has provided a unique perspective on the world's best travel destinations by using specially commissioned photography and illuminating text written by local authors.

Whether you're planning a city break, a walking tour or the journey of a lifetime, our superb range of guidebooks and phrasebooks will inspire you to discover more about your chosen destination.

INSIGHT GUIDES

offer a unique combination of stunning photos, absorbing narrative and detailed maps, providing all the inspiration and information you need.

PHRASEBOOKS & DICTIONARIES

help users to feel at home, when away. Pocket-sized with a free app to download, they go where you do.

CITY GUIDES

pack hundreds of great photos into a smaller format with detailed practical information, so you can navigate the world's top cities with confidence.

EXPLORE GUIDES

feature easy-to-follow walks and itineraries in the world's most exciting destinations, with our choice of the best places to eat and drink along the way.

POCKET GUIDES

combine concise information on where to go and what to do in a handy compact format, ideal on the ground. Includes a full-colour, fold-out map.

EXPERIENCE GUIDES

feature offbeat perspectives and secret gems for experienced travellers, with a collection of over 100 ideas for a memorable stay in a city.

www.insightguides.com